THE AMAZING BIG BOOK OF FUN FACTS

Explore Over 1500 Fascinating Facts
About the World, Food, Animals,
Space and Beyond!

Milo Brightstone

CONTENTS

INTRODUCTION

Welcome to the World of Awesome Facts!

Hi there, curious minds! Have you ever wondered why the ocean is so deep or how big dinosaurs really were? Or maybe you're fascinated by what it would be like to live in space or discover the ancient secrets of lost cities.

 If so, this book is for you! Inside, you'll find amazing facts that will take you on an adventure from the tallest mountains to the bottom of the ocean, and even far beyond our galaxy.
Every chapter brings you closer to something extraordinary!

 You'll learn about:

- Animals with Super Skills: Did you know that some animals can grow back lost body parts, taste with their feet, or jump 200 times their body length?

- Space and Stars: What's beyond our planet? Are there planets made of diamonds? What would it be like to live on Mars?

- The Secrets of Our Bodies: How does your brain help you remember? Are humans teeth stronger than that of a shark? And did you know that your heart is a powerful little pump?

- Incredible Inventions: Some inventions make our lives easier, while others changed the world in ways no one expected. What are the wild stories behind them?

- Ocean Mysteries: Did you know we've only explored a tiny part of the ocean? What strange creatures are waiting in the deep?

You'll also discover strange weather, hidden jungles, and ancient civilizations that shaped the world we live in today. Plus, there are record-breaking plants and animals, and even creepy-crawlies with amazing abilities!

This book will help you uncover answers to questions like:

- How do plants survive in places where it barely rains?

- What's it like to go back in time to the age of dinosaurs or visit faraway planets?

- What's the weirdest weather on Earth, and where can you find it?

Each chapter has surprises that will leave you saying, "Wow, I never knew that!" Whether it's learning about animals that can glow in the dark, facts about foods that come from far-off lands, or mysteries that scientists are still trying to solve, this book will inspire you to keep exploring and asking questions.

Are you ready to dive in? Turn the page and let's set off on a journey filled with facts that will surprise, entertain, and maybe even make you laugh.

From record-breaking animals to hidden mysteries of the mind, there's a whole world of wonders waiting for you to discover!

AMAZING
ANIMALS

ANIMAL ADAPTATIONS

- Octopuses have three hearts – two pump blood to the gills, and one pumps it to the rest of the body.

- Camels have three eyelids to protect their eyes from sand.

- Some frogs can freeze in winter and come back to life when they thaw.

- Elephants use their trunks as a snorkel when swimming in deep water.

- Sharks never run out of teeth; they can lose thousands in a lifetime and grow new ones.

- Giraffes have tongues up to 20 inches long to help them reach leaves.

- Cats can rotate their ears 180 degrees, allowing them to hear from every direction.

- A rhinoceros beetle can carry 850 times its own weight — like a human lifting 65 tons!

- Bats are the only mammals that can truly fly.

- Armadillos can hold their breath for up to six minutes while digging.

ANIMAL SENSES

- Eagles can spot prey from over two miles away, thanks to their highly focused eyesight and large pupils that let in ample light.

- Elephants detect seismic vibrations through their feet.

- Some snakes, like pit vipers, use infrared pits to "see" heat, making them expert hunters even in complete darkness.

- A dog's nose is up to 100,000 times more sensitive than ours.

- Dolphins "see" with sound by emitting clicks and listening for echoes, allowing them to navigate murky waters and locate prey.

- Butterflies taste plants with their feet to find suitable spots for eggs.

- Asymmetrical ears help owls locate sounds in the dark.

- Sharks detect electric fields using special organs.

- Mantis shrimp have some of the most complex eyes on Earth, seeing ultraviolet, polarized light, and a broader range of colors than humans.

- Cats' whiskers sense air currents and help them navigate in the dark.

STRANGE ANIMAL HOMES

- Termite mounds can be over 20 feet tall, as big as a small building.

- Beavers build dams to create ponds for protection from predators.

- Hermit crabs "borrow" shells from other animals to use as their home.

- Clownfish live in sea anemones, which sting most other fish.

- Prairie dogs dig huge underground tunnels with separate "rooms."

- Birds called swifts spend almost their entire life in the air, even sleeping while flying.

- Ants build complex colonies that can extend underground and hold millions of ants.

- Coral reefs are actually made by tiny animals called coral polyps.

- Owls make nests in trees, cliffs, and even cacti!

- Spider webs are both homes and traps for food for spiders.

RECORD BREAKING ANIMALS

- The cheetah is the fastest land animal, reaching speeds of 70 mph.

- Blue whales are the largest animals on Earth, bigger than the biggest dinosaurs.

- The peregrine falcon is the fastest bird, diving at over 200 mph.

- The Arctic tern has the longest migration — flying from the North Pole to the South Pole.

- The giant squid has the largest eyes of any animal, up to 10 inches across.

- The longest-living land animal is the Aldabra giant tortoise, which can live over 150 years.

- Box jellyfish have as many as 24 eyes, though they don't have a brain.

- Giraffes are the tallest land animals, reaching up to 18 feet.

- The male seahorse carries the babies, making it the only animal where the dad is "pregnant."

- Elephants have the longest pregnancy, lasting about 22 months!

ANIMAL DIETS AND FOOD

- Pandas eat almost only bamboo — up to 99% of their diet.

- Some ants "farm" aphids for food, much like humans raise animals.

- Kangaroos chew food, swallow, and then regurgitate it to chew again.

- Vultures have extremely strong stomach acids to help digest rotting meat.

- Koalas eat eucalyptus leaves, which are toxic to most animals.

- Opossums are immune to snake venom, allowing them to eat poisonous snakes.

- A honeybee can fly up to six miles to find food.

- Octopuses eat by drilling holes in shells and using their beaks to suck out the prey.

- Whales eat millions of tiny shrimp-like krill instead of larger fish.

- The African elephant eats up to 600 pounds of food per day.

ANIMAL COMMUNICATION

- Whales use "songs" to communicate across long distances.

- Bees perform a "waggle dance" to show others where food is located.

- Elephants "rumble" to communicate with others miles away.

- Dolphins have names for each other, using unique whistles.

- Birds sing to claim territory and attract mates.

- Ants leave scent trails to guide others to food.

- Dogs wag their tails not just in happiness but for various emotions

- Wolves howl to communicate with the pack and establish territory.

- Male frogs sing to attract female frogs.

- Cats use different meows to "talk" to humans, though they rarely meow at each other.

UNUSUAL ABILITIES

- Salamanders can regrow lost limbs like tails and even parts of their heart.

- Sea stars can regrow lost arms and sometimes whole new bodies.

- Hummingbirds are the only birds that can fly backward.

- Alpacas and llamas spit when they feel threatened.

- Some fish can change gender as part of their life cycle.

- Octopuses can squeeze through tiny spaces as long as their beak fits.

- Electric eels can generate electricity to shock predators or catch prey.

- The bombardier beetle sprays boiling chemicals to scare off enemies.

- Axolotls can regenerate their spinal cord if it's damaged.

- Penguins can drink salt water, filtering it through special glands.

FUN ANIMAL FACTS

- Polar bears have black skin under their white fur to absorb heat.

- A group of flamingos is called a "flamboyance."

- Dolphins have unique "names" they use to call each other.

- Tigers' skin is striped, just like their fur.

- Kangaroos can't walk backward.

- Goats have rectangular pupils to help them see 360 degrees.

- A snail can sleep for three years if conditions are bad.

- Otters hold hands while they sleep to keep from drifting apart.

- Cows have best friends and can get stressed when separated.

- Rats laugh when tickled.

ANIMAL LIFESPANS

- The Greenland shark can live over 400 years.

- Parrots can live for more than 60 years.

- A mayfly has the shortest lifespan, sometimes only living for a day.

- Queen termites can live for 25 to 50 years.

- Lobsters might live forever if not caught due to endless cell repair.

ANIMAL SURVIVAL SKILLS

- Sea cucumbers can expel their intestines to scare off predators.

- Kangaroo rats can live without water for their entire life.

- The mimic octopus can impersonate other animals like lionfish or flatfish.

- Horses sleep standing up to be ready to escape quickly.

- Butterflies can fool predators with eye spots on their wings.

MISCELLANEOUS MARVELS

- Koalas have fingerprints that are similar to humans.

- Baby elephants suck their trunks for comfort, like human babies with thumbs.

- Horses and cows sleep lying down only for short periods.

- Cats have 30 teeth, while dogs have 42.

- Octopuses can change their skin color for camouflage.

- Ducks sleep with one eye open.

- Camels can drink up to 40 gallons of water in one go.

- Starfish have no brains or blood but use seawater to pump nutrients.

- Some fish "walk" on land using fins.

- Sloths move so slowly that algae can grow on their fur, camouflaging them.

SPACE AND BEYOND

OUR SOLAR SYSTEM

- The Sun is over 1 million times bigger than Earth!

- Mercury is the closest planet to the Sun, but Venus is the hottest due to its thick atmosphere.

- A day on Venus is longer than a year on Venus – it rotates very slowly!

- Earth is the only planet with liquid water on its surface that we know of.

- Mars has the largest volcano in our solar system, called Olympus Mons—it's three times taller than Mount Everest.

- Jupiter has a storm called the Great Red Spot, which has been raging for at least 300 years.

- Saturn's rings are made of ice, rock, and dust—some pieces are as big as a house!

- Uranus rotates on its side, unlike any other planet in the solar system.

- Neptune has winds faster than any other planet, reaching speeds over 1,200 mph.

- Pluto used to be the ninth planet, but it's now classified as a "dwarf planet."

THE SUN AND STARS

- The Sun's core is about 27 million degrees Fahrenheit.

- Stars come in different colors based on their temperature – blue stars are the hottest, and red stars are the coolest.

- The closest star to Earth (after the Sun) is Proxima Centauri, about 4.24 light-years away.

- A supernova is the explosion of a star, which can be brighter than an entire galaxy for a short time.

- Our Sun will eventually become a red giant, growing large enough to possibly engulf Earth.

- Neutron stars are so dense that a sugar-cube-sized piece would weigh about a billion tons!

- A star's color can tell us its age and temperature – younger, hotter stars are blue; older, cooler stars are red.

- Stars can live for billions of years, depending on their size.

- The Sun is a medium-sized star known as a yellow dwarf.

- The energy from the Sun's core takes about 170,000 years to reach its surface!

THE MOON

- The Moon has no atmosphere, so there's no weather or sound.

- The Moon always shows the same face to Earth because it rotates at the same rate it orbits us.

- Footprints on the Moon could last for millions of years, as there's no wind to erase them.

- The Moon is slowly moving away from Earth at a rate of about 1.5 inches per year.

- There's evidence of ice in permanently shadowed craters on the Moon.

- The Moon has "seas" called maria, but they are made of hardened lava, not water.

- During a lunar eclipse, Earth's shadow can turn the Moon a reddish color, known as a "Blood Moon."

- The Moon is about 4.5 billion years old, just a little younger than Earth.

- Some scientists think the Moon was formed when a giant object hit Earth billions of years ago.

- Tides on Earth are caused by the gravitational pull of the Moon and the Sun.

SPACE EXPLORATION

- The first man in space was Yuri Gagarin from Russia in 1961.

- The first American astronaut to orbit Earth was John Glenn, in 1962.

- Neil Armstrong and Buzz Aldrin were the first humans to walk on the Moon in 1969.

- NASA's Voyager 1 spacecraft is the farthest human-made object from Earth.

- Mars rovers, like Curiosity, have been exploring Mars to learn about its history and climate.

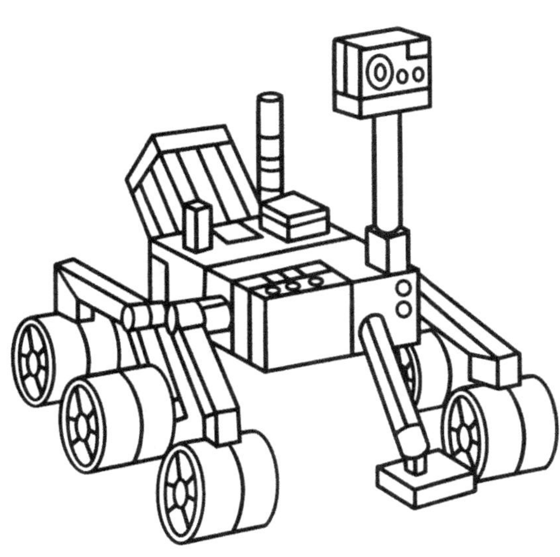

- The International Space Station (ISS) orbits Earth at about 17,500 miles per hour.

- Astronauts on the ISS see a sunrise or sunset every 90 minutes.

- The Hubble Space Telescope orbits Earth and has captured some of the most detailed images of space.

- The Parker Solar Probe is the closest spacecraft to the Sun, reaching within 4 million miles.

- SpaceX, a private company, launched the first manned commercial flight to the ISS in 2020.

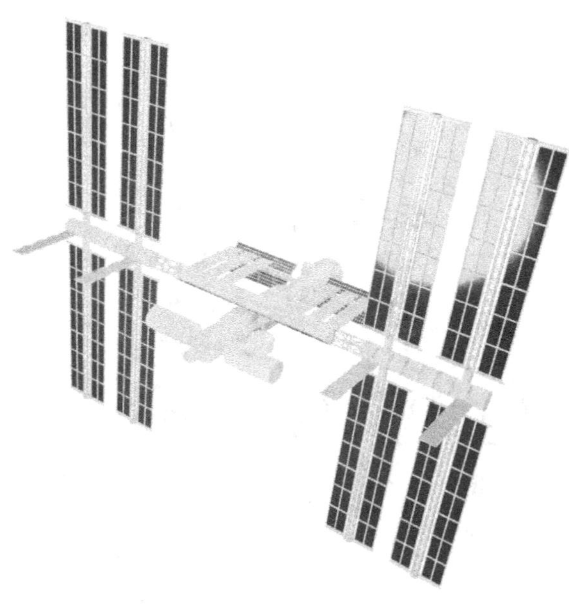

THE MILKY WAY GALAXY

- Our galaxy, the Milky Way, is a barred spiral galaxy with a black hole at its center.

- The Milky Way has hundreds of billions of stars.

- It takes the Sun about 225 million years to orbit the center of the Milky Way.

- Our galaxy is part of a group of galaxies called the Local Group.

- The Milky Way will collide with the nearby Andromeda Galaxy in about 4.5 billion years.

- The Milky Way is about 100,000 light-years across.

- Our solar system is located in one of the Milky Way's spiral arms called the Orion Arm.

- The center of the Milky Way is full of dense gas and dust, making it hard to see through.

- Most of the stars in the Milky Way are red dwarfs, which are smaller and cooler than our Sun.

- Scientists use radio waves to study the center of the Milky Way, as visible light can't penetrate the dust clouds.

BLACK HOLES

- A black hole is formed when a massive star collapses after a supernova.

- Black holes have such strong gravity that nothing, not even light, can escape.

- Some black holes are billions of times more massive than the Sun.

- Quasars are extremely bright objects powered by black holes in the centers of galaxies.

- Wormholes are theoretical "tunnels" in space-time that could connect distant places.

- The nearest known black hole to Earth is about 1,500 light-years away.

- Black holes can "spaghettify" objects, stretching them into long strings.

- There may be "mini" black holes smaller than atoms, though none have been found.

- Some scientists think wormholes could exist, but none have been found.

- The biggest known black hole is 40 billion times the mass of the Sun.

COMETS, ASTEROIDS, METEORS

- Comets are made of ice, dust, and rock and have tails that glow when they get close to the Sun.

- The famous comet Halley's Comet returns every 76 years.

- Asteroids are rocky objects that orbit the Sun, mostly found in the asteroid belt.

- Meteors are pieces of debris that burn up in Earth's atmosphere, creating shooting stars.

- The largest asteroid, Ceres, is also classified as a dwarf planet.

- A meteorite is a meteor that reaches Earth's surface.

- The Chicxulub impact, an asteroid that hit Earth 66 million years ago, is believed to have caused the dinosaurs' extinction.

- Comet tails always point away from the Sun, pushed by solar wind.

- The asteroid belt between Mars and Jupiter contains millions of rocky objects.

- Meteor showers happen when Earth passes through a comet's debris.

BEYOND OUR SOLAR SYSTEM

- There are more stars in the universe than grains of sand on all Earth's beaches.

- Some stars have planets orbiting them, known as exoplanets.

- The closest exoplanet to us is Proxima Centauri b, located about 4.24 light-years away.

- Super-Earths are planets bigger than Earth but smaller than Neptune.

- Some planets outside our solar system might have two suns, like Tatooine in "Star Wars"!

- Scientists think there could be life on some exoplanets with conditions similar to Earth.

- A light-year is the distance light travels in one year, about 5.88 trillion miles.

- The largest known star, UY Scuti, is about 1,700 times bigger than the Sun.

- Some exoplanets orbit their stars in just a few hours!

- There could be billions of habitable planets in our galaxy alone.

DARK MATTER AND ENERGY

- Dark matter makes up about 85% of the universe's mass, but we can't see it.

- Dark energy is believed to be causing the universe to expand faster.

- Scientists still don't know what dark matter and dark energy really are.

- Dark matter doesn't emit or absorb light, which makes it invisible.

- Some galaxies may be made almost entirely of dark matter.

FUN SPACE FACTS

- A day on Mars is just 37 minutes longer than a day on Earth.

- Saturn's moon Titan has rivers and lakes of liquid methane.

- A year on Mercury is only 88 Earth days long.

- Venus spins backward compared to most planets.

- Astronauts on the ISS feel weightless due to free-fall.

- Neptune has 14 known moons.

- There's a hexagonal storm on Saturn's north pole.

- Enceladus, one of Saturn's moons, has geysers of water.

- Mars has two moons: Phobos and Deimos.

- The surface of Venus is hot enough to melt lead.

- Uranus has a faint ring system.

- The Oort Cloud is a vast, icy region surrounding our solar system.

- Space is almost a perfect vacuum.

- Sound can't travel in space due to the lack of air.

- Astronauts in space age slower than people on Earth due to relativity.

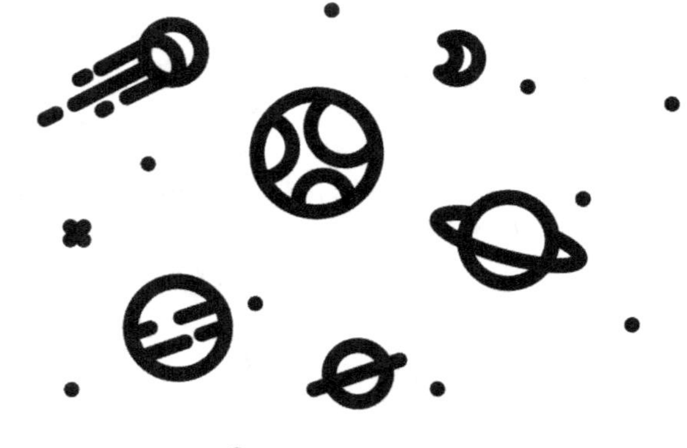

THE HUMAN BODY

BONES AND SKELETON

- The human body has 206 bones, but babies are born with about 300!

- The smallest bone in your body is in your ear, called the stapes, and it's only 0.1 inches long.

- Your bones are five times stronger than steel of the same density.

- Over half of your bones are in your hands and feet.

- The longest bone in your body is the femur, or thigh bone, which is about a quarter of your height.

- Bones are constantly being broken down and rebuilt, which means they are "alive."

- The hyoid bone in your neck is the only bone not connected to any other bone.

- The skull has 22 bones, which protect your brain.

- Bones stop growing after puberty, but they continue to change shape throughout your life.

- Bones are filled with a spongy material called bone marrow, which makes blood cells.

MUSCLES AND MOVEMENT

- The human body has over 600 muscles.

- Your strongest muscle, relative to size, is the masseter, or jaw muscle.

- The gluteus maximus, or buttocks muscle, is the largest muscle in your body.

- The smallest muscles are in your inner ear and are responsible for helping you hear.

- It takes 17 muscles to smile and 43 muscles to frown (so smiling is easier!).

- Your heart is also a muscle and beats about 100,000 times a day.

- Eye muscles are the most active muscles in your body and can move over 100,000 times a day.

- Shivering is your body's way of trying to stay warm by quickly contracting muscles.

- The tongue is the only muscle attached at just one end, making it very flexible.

- It takes around 200 muscles just to take a single step!

THE BRAIN AND NERVOUS SYSTEM

- Your brain is about 60% fat—it's the fattiest organ in your body.

- The brain has around 86 billion neurons, which are cells that help it process information.

- You can't tickle yourself because your brain anticipates the touch.

- Neurons in your brain send messages at speeds up to 200 miles per hour.

- The human brain can store about 2.5 petabytes of information, similar to a million gigabytes.

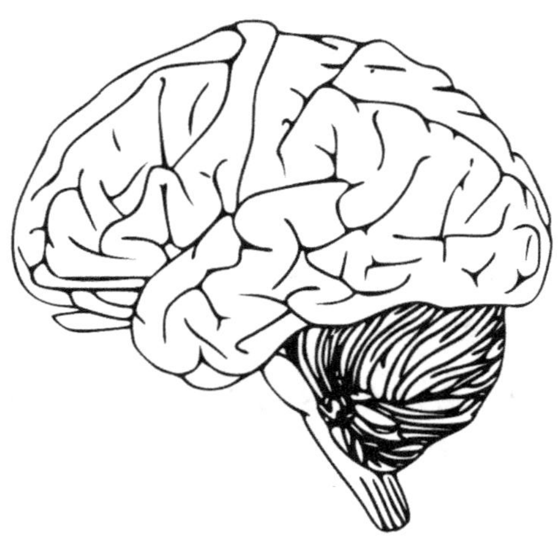

- Your brain uses about 20% of your body's energy, even though it's only 2% of your weight.

- During REM sleep, your brain is almost as active as when you're awake.

- Your brain creates enough electricity to power a small light bulb.

- The left side of your brain controls the right side of your body, and vice versa.

- Humans use more than 10% of their brains—this is a myth; nearly all parts have a function.

THE HEART AND CIRCULATORY SYSTEM

- Your heart beats around 3 billion times in a lifetime.

- The heart pumps about 1.5 gallons of blood every minute.

- Your blood vessels are over 60,000 miles long, enough to circle the Earth twice!

- Red blood cells are made in the bone marrow and live for about 120 days.

- There are about 5 liters of blood in the average adult body.

- Blood makes up about 8% of your body weight.

- Your heart beats faster when you're excited or scared to pump more blood to your muscles.

- Each red blood cell completes a circuit around your body in about 20 seconds.

- The "lub-dub" sound of your heart is from valves closing to prevent blood from flowing backward.

- Blood is red because of the iron in hemoglobin, which carries oxygen.

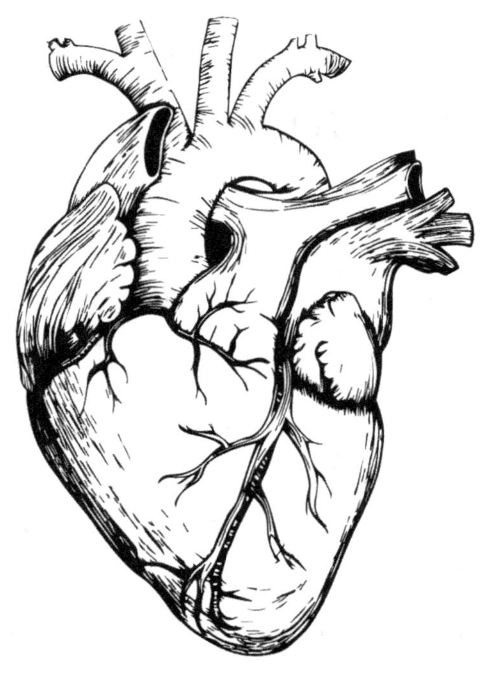

THE DIGESTIVE SYSTEM

- Your stomach has a very strong acid called hydrochloric acid, which helps digest food.

- The average person produces 1 to 3 pints of saliva every day.

- Your small intestine is about 20 feet long, much longer than your height!

- It takes food about 6 to 8 hours to pass through your stomach and small intestine.

- The large intestine absorbs water and forms solid waste.

- Your stomach lining is replaced every 3 to 4 days to protect against acid.

- Burping releases trapped air from your stomach.

- There are millions of bacteria in your gut, many of which help digest food.

- The liver is the largest internal organ and performs over 500 functions.

- The average person passes gas about 14 times a day—it's a normal part of digestion.

THE RESPIRATORY SYSTEM

- Humans breathe about 12-16 times per minute.

- The right lung is slightly larger than the left lung because of the heart's position.

- The surface area of your lungs is about the size of a tennis court.

- Your diaphragm is a muscle that helps you breathe by moving up and down.

- The nose has small hairs called cilia that filter dust and other particles.

- The airways in your lungs are called bronchi and bronchioles.
- Yawning helps bring more oxygen into the blood.

- When you sneeze, air leaves your body at speeds of up to 100 mph.

- Lungs contain about 300 million tiny air sacs called alveoli.

- Hiccups are caused by involuntary contractions of the diaphragm.

SKIN AND HAIR

- The skin is the body's largest organ.

- You shed about 30,000-40,000 skin cells every minute.

- The average person has about 5 million hair follicles.

- Human hair is as strong as a wire of iron of the same diameter.

- The skin renews itself every 28 days.

- The color of your skin is determined by melanin.

- Your fingerprints are unique, even in identical twins.

- Goosebumps are caused by tiny muscles at the base of hair follicles contracting.

- Nails grow faster in the summer than in the winter.

- The thickest skin on your body is on the soles of your feet.

THE SENSES

- The average person blinks about 15-20 times per minute.

- Taste buds aren't just on your tongue—they're also on the roof of your mouth and throat.

- Humans can see millions of different colors.

- Ears help you balance as well as hear.

- The sense of smell is linked closely to memory.

- Eyes can distinguish about 10 million different colors.

- The lens in your eye changes shape to focus on objects.

- You have about 10,000 taste buds, which decrease as you get older.

- Your sense of smell can detect over a trillion scents.

- The average person can detect about 500,000 different sounds.

BLOOD

- The average human has about 5 liters of blood flowing through their body.

- Blood travels approximately 12,000 miles every day inside your body.

- There are four main blood types: A, B, AB, and O.

- People with O-negative blood are universal donors and can donate to anyone.

- Blood is made in the soft marrow inside your bones.

- Red blood cells carry oxygen to your body and remove carbon dioxide.

- There are about 25 trillion red blood cells in your body at any given time.

- Red blood cells live for around 120 days before being replaced.

- White blood cells fight germs and infections in your body.

- Plasma, the yellow liquid part of blood, makes up more than half of its volume.

WONDERFUL BODY FACTS

- Your brain is about the size of two fists together.

- You have as many hairs on your body as a chimpanzee, though most are fine and invisible.

- Humans are the only animals that blush.

- Your stomach "growls" when gas and fluid move through it.

- People grow slightly taller in the morning than at night due to spine compression.

- The liver can regenerate and regrow even if a large part is removed.

- Human teeth are just as strong as shark teeth.

- Human bodies produce enough saliva each day to fill a small water bottle.

- Your taste buds replace themselves about every 10 days.

- You're about 1% shorter in the evening than in the morning, due to gravity compressing your spine.

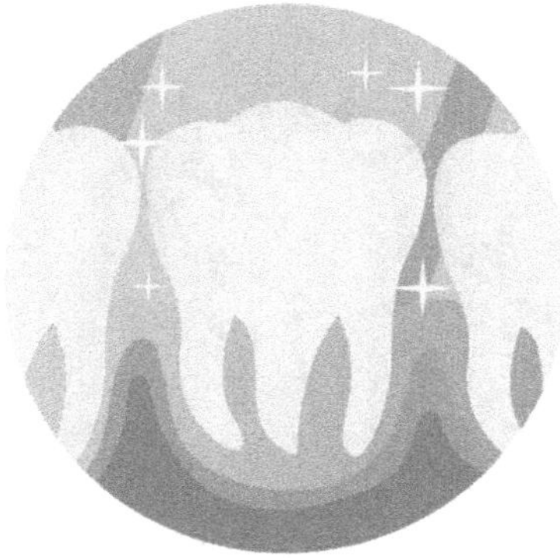

GROWTH AND DEVELOPMENT

- Babies are born with 300 bones, but some fuse together as they grow.

- Newborns don't have kneecaps—they develop them as they grow.

- Your ears and nose never stop growing throughout your life.

- Every cell in your body is replaced every 7 to 10 years.

- You grow faster in spring and summer than in winter.

- Your body is about 70% water..

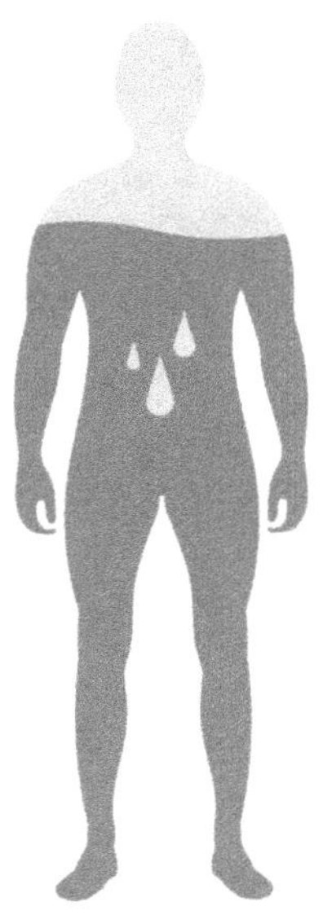

- Babies blink less than adults because they don't need to protect their eyes as much.

- Most babies are born with blue or gray eyes, but the color may change with time.

- Humans have unique fingerprints, even as babies.

- Your nails grow faster on your dominant hand.

INCREDIBLE INVENTIONS

ANCIENT INVENTIONS

- The wheel was invented around 3500 BCE in Mesopotamia.

- Papyrus, the first type of paper, was invented by the ancient Egyptians around 3000 BCE.

- The abacus, an ancient counting tool, was used as early as 2400 BCE.

- The first known toothbrush was created in China in the 15th century and was made from animal hair.

- The ancient Greeks invented the concept of plumbing over 2,000 years ago.

- Concrete was invented by the ancient Romans, and some of their structures still stand today.

- The first known battery, the Baghdad Battery, was invented over 2,000 years ago.

- The compass was invented in ancient China over 2,000 years ago to aid in navigation.

- The ancient Egyptians invented ink for writing around 2500 BCE.

- The first flush toilets were invented by the Minoans on the island of Crete, over 4,000 years ago.

TRANSPORTATION BREAKTHROUGHS

- The first bicycle was invented in 1817 by Karl Drais, a German baron.

- The Wright brothers invented the first successful airplane in 1903.

- The first automobile was invented by Karl Benz in 1886 and had three wheels.

- The steam engine, which powered trains and factories, was invented in the 18th century.

- The first hot air balloon flight took place in France in 1783.

- The electric car was first invented in the 1830s, long before gasoline cars became popular.

- The first submarine was invented in 1620 by Cornelius Drebbel, a Dutch engineer.

- The first helicopter was designed by Igor Sikorsky and successfully flew in 1939.

- Trains were initially powered by horses before steam engines came along.

- The first modern passenger elevator was invented by Elisha Otis in 1857.

COMMUNICATION REVOLUTION

- The first printing press was invented by Johannes Gutenberg around 1440.

- The first telegraph, created by Samuel Morse in 1837, allowed instant communication over long distances.

- Alexander Graham Bell invented the telephone in 1876, transforming communication.

- The radio was invented by Guglielmo Marconi in the 1890s, allowing people to broadcast sound.

- Television was invented in the 1920s, changing the way people consumed news and entertainment.

- The first email was sent in 1971, marking the start of digital communication.

- The first typewriter was patented in 1868 and looked very different from modern keyboards.

- Cell phones were invented in 1973 by Martin Cooper.

- The Internet was invented in the 1960s as a government project in the United States.

- The first social media platform, Six Degrees, was created in 1997.

MEDICAL MARVELS

- Vaccination was first discovered in 1796 by Edward Jenner to protect against smallpox.

- The X-ray was invented by Wilhelm Röntgen in 1895, allowing doctors to see inside the human body.

- The stethoscope was invented in 1816 by René Laennec to listen to heartbeats and breathing.

- Penicillin, the first antibiotic, was discovered in 1928 by Alexander Fleming.

- The first successful organ transplant was a kidney transplant in 1954.

- Anaesthesia, which makes surgeries painless, was first used in 1846.

- The first MRI machine, used to scan the body, was created in 1977.

- Eyeglasses were invented in the 13th century to help people see better.

- The pacemaker, a device that helps the heart beat correctly, was invented in 1950.

- The thermometer, used to measure temperature, was invented by Galileo in 1593.

COMPUTER AND DIGITAL AGE

- The first computer was invented in 1945 and was as big as a room.

- The first hard drive, made in 1956, could only hold 5 megabytes of data.

- The mouse for computers was invented by Douglas Engelbart in 1964.

- The first video game was invented in 1958 and was a simple tennis game.

- The World Wide Web was invented by Tim Berners-Lee in 1989, changing the Internet forever.

- The USB, invented in 1995, made it easy to store and transfer files.

- The first smartphone was released by IBM in 1994.

- The emoji was invented in Japan in the 1990s as a way to add emotion to messages.

- The first computer virus was created in 1983 as an experiment.

- Artificial Intelligence (AI) started gaining popularity in the 1950s.

FOOD AND COOKING GADGETS

- Instant noodles were invented in 1958 in Japan and became a global favorite.

- The ice cream maker was invented in 1843 by Nancy Johnson.

- The first electric blender was invented in 1922 by Stephen Poplawski.

- Canned food was invented in 1810 to preserve food for soldiers.

- The coffee maker was invented in 1908 by Melitta Bentz in Germany.

- The soda can was patented in 1936, making it easy to store and transport drinks.

- The first food processor was invented in 1973 by Pierre Verdon.

- Bubble gum was invented in 1928 by Walter Diemer.

- Potato chips were invented by accident in 1853 by chef George Crum.

- The toaster was invented in 1893 to quickly brown bread.

TOYS AND ENTERTAINMENT

- LEGO bricks were invented in 1958 and have since become a favorite toy worldwide.

- The first video game console, the Magnavox Odyssey, was released in 1972.

- The Frisbee was invented in 1957 by Walter Morrison.

- The yo-yo is one of the oldest toys, dating back over 2,500 years.

- The Rubik's Cube was invented in 1974 by Erno Rubik, a Hungarian architect.

- The skateboard was invented in the 1950s, inspired by surfing.

- Silly Putty was accidentally invented in 1943 when trying to make synthetic rubber.

- Play-Doh was originally created in the 1930s as wallpaper cleaner.

- The hula hoop became popular in the 1950s after it was invented by Wham-O.

- The slinky was invented in 1943 by accident when a spring fell off a shelf.

CLOTHING AND FASHION

- The sewing machine was invented by Elias Howe in 1846, transforming clothing production.

- Blue jeans were invented by Levi Strauss in 1873.

- The first wristwatch was created in 1868 for a Hungarian countess.

- Sunglasses were invented in China over 800 years ago to protect from the sun.

- Velcro was invented in 1941 by George de Mestral after observing burrs sticking to his clothes.

- The safety helmet was invented in 1914 to protect workers and athletes.

- Contact lenses were first designed in 1888.

- Silk comes from silk worm cocoons, which are spun into thread.

- Elastic bands were invented in 1845 and are used in clothing and various items.

- The zipper was invented in 1893, making fastening easier.

HOUSEHOLD INNOVATIONS

- The vacuum cleaner was invented in 1901 to help people clean their homes.

- The first electric light bulb was invented by Thomas Edison in 1879.

- The refrigerator was invented in the 1830s, making food storage easier and safer.

- The first washing machine was invented in the 1850s, changing laundry forever.

- The first microwave oven was invented in 1945 by Percy Spencer.

- The safety pin was invented by Walter Hunt in 1849.

- Aluminum foil, invented in 1910, became popular for food storage.

- Paper towels were invented by accident in 1907.

- The zipper was invented in 1893 by Whitcomb Judson to fasten clothes easily.

- The dishwasher was invented in 1886 by Josephine Cochrane.

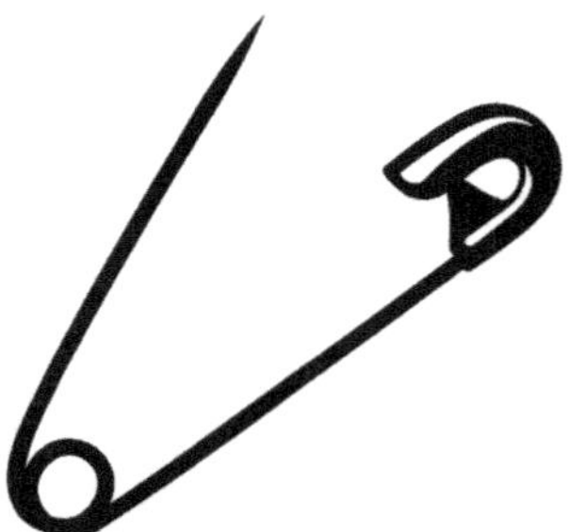

ENVIRONMENTAL INNOVATIONS

- The first solar cell was invented in 1954 to harness energy from the sun.

- Plastic recycling was developed in the 1970s to reduce waste.

- The electric car was reinvented in the 1990s to reduce pollution.

- Composting, an ancient practice, is an early invention to recycle food waste.

- Wind turbines were invented in the 1800s to generate energy from the wind.

- Recycled paper was first made in the early 20th century to save trees.

- Biodegradable plastics were invented in the 1980s to reduce waste.

- The first reusable water bottle was created in the 1970s.

- Solar-powered calculators were invented in the 1980s as an eco-friendly tool.

- The electric bus was introduced in the early 2000s to reduce air pollution.

OCEAN WONDERS

OCEAN BASICS

- Oceans cover more than 70% of Earth's surface.

- There are five major oceans: the Pacific, Atlantic, Indian, Southern, and Arctic.

- The Pacific Ocean is the largest ocean, covering about 63 million square miles.

- The ocean contains around 97% of Earth's water.

- The average depth of the ocean is about 12,100 feet.

- The Mariana Trench is the deepest part of the ocean, reaching 36,000 feet deep.

- Around 80% of the ocean is unexplored by humans.

- The ocean produces more than half of the oxygen we breathe.

- The Atlantic Ocean is growing each year due to tectonic plates moving apart.

- The Pacific Ocean is shrinking as tectonic plates push it together.

INCREDIBLE MARINE LIFE

- Blue whales are the largest animals on Earth, reaching up to 100 feet in length.

- Jellyfish have existed for over 500 million years, making them older than dinosaurs.

- Giant squids can grow up to 40 feet long and have eyes the size of basketballs.

- Octopuses have three hearts and blue blood.

- Dolphins are incredibly intelligent and can communicate with each other using clicks and whistles.

- Sea turtles have been around for over 100 million years.

- The ocean is home to bioluminescent creatures that glow in the dark.

- The mantis shrimp can punch with the force of a bullet, breaking shells and even aquarium glass.

- The whale shark is the largest fish in the ocean, growing up to 40 feet long.

- Some species of seahorses mate for life, and males carry the babies.

OCEAN LAYERS AND ZONES

- The ocean is divided into different layers or zones based on depth.

- The sunlight zone is the top layer, where most marine life lives.

- The twilight zone is darker and home to strange creatures like lanternfish.

- The midnight zone has no sunlight and is home to creatures that create their own light.

- The abyssal zone is extremely deep, dark, and cold.

- The hadal zone is found in deep trenches and is home to very few, hardy organisms.

- Most life in the ocean lives within the sunlight zone, up to 650 feet deep.

- Coral reefs are mostly found in shallow, warm parts of the sunlight zone.

- Only specialized creatures can survive the crushing pressure of deep ocean zones.

- The midnight and abyssal zones cover about 90% of the ocean.

CORAL REEFS

- Coral reefs are made up of tiny creatures called polyps.

- Coral reefs support about 25% of all marine species.

- The Great Barrier Reef in Australia is the largest coral reef in the world.

- Corals get their bright colors from algae that live inside them.

- Coral reefs are sometimes called the "rainforests of the sea".

- Coral reefs are threatened by climate change and pollution.

- Some coral reefs are over 10,000 years old.

- Coral reefs protect coastlines from storms by absorbing wave energy.

- Many fish species rely on coral reefs for food and shelter.

- When coral reefs die, it's known as "coral bleaching".

OCEAN TIDES AND WAVES

- Tides are caused by the gravitational pull of the moon and the sun.

- There are usually two high tides and two low tides each day.

- Waves are created by wind blowing across the surface of the water.

- The highest waves can reach over 100 feet.

- Tsunamis are huge waves caused by underwater earthquakes.

- Rip currents are strong, narrow currents that can pull swimmers out to sea.

- The biggest recorded wave reached 1,720 feet after a landslide in Alaska.

- Some animals use the tides to time their activities, like feeding and nesting.

- Surfers look for specific types of waves called swells.

- Seawater moves in giant circular currents called gyres.

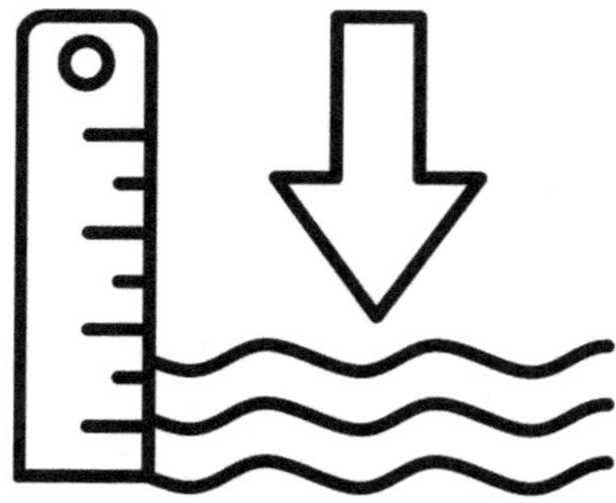

MARINE MAMMALS

- Whales, dolphins, and seals are all marine mammals.

- Marine mammals breathe air and need to surface to get oxygen.

- Sperm whales can dive more than a mile deep to hunt for food.

- Orcas, also known as killer whales, are actually dolphins.

- Dolphins use echolocation to find food and navigate.

- Some seals can hold their breath for over an hour while diving.

- Humpback whales sing long, complex songs to communicate.

- Walruses have large tusks that help them climb out of the water.

- Manatees, also known as sea cows, are gentle herbivores.

- The narwhal, called the "unicorn of the sea," has a long tusk that can grow up to 10 feet.

SURPRISING CREATURES

- The anglerfish has a glowing lure on its head to attract prey in the dark ocean depths.

- The vampire squid can turn itself inside out to avoid predators.

- The blobfish is considered one of the ugliest animals due to its squishy appearance.

- The ocean sunfish is one of the heaviest bony fish, weighing up to 5,000 pounds.

- The giant isopod is a large, deep-sea crustacean that looks like a giant pill bug.

- The gulper eel can swallow prey much larger than itself thanks to its big mouth.

- The deep-sea dragonfish has sharp teeth and glowing spots to attract prey.

- The leafy sea dragon looks like floating seaweed to hide from predators.

- The cookiecutter shark bites circular chunks out of its prey.

- The Portuguese man o' war is not a single animal but a colony of different organisms.

OCEAN ECOSYSTEMS

- Kelp forests grow along coastlines and provide shelter for many sea creatures.

- Mangroves, which grow in salty water, help protect coastlines from erosion.

- Seagrass meadows are one of the few underwater plants and provide habitat for marine life.

- Salt marshes act as natural filters, trapping pollutants before they reach the ocean.

- Some fish, like salmon, travel from the ocean to freshwater to spawn.

- Estuaries are areas where rivers meet the ocean and are rich in nutrients.

- Coral reefs, kelp forests, and seagrass meadows are the "big three" ocean habitats.

- Ocean ecosystems are very delicate and can be easily disrupted by pollution.

- Plankton, tiny ocean organisms, are the base of the marine food chain.

- Some fish, like clownfish, live in partnership with sea anemones for protection.

OCEAN CONSERVATION

- Plastic pollution is a big threat to ocean life, harming animals who mistake it for food.

- Overfishing has reduced fish populations, threatening ocean biodiversity.

- Many marine animals are endangered due to human activities.

- Marine reserves are protected areas where ocean life can thrive without human interference.

- Reducing single-use plastics can help protect ocean creatures from eating or getting trapped in plastic.

- Coral reefs are particularly sensitive to rising ocean temperatures.

- Using less fossil fuel helps reduce ocean acidification, which harms marine life.

- Whale watching can support conservation if done responsibly.

- The Great Pacific Garbage Patch is a huge area of floating plastic waste.

- Supporting sustainable seafood choices helps protect ocean ecosystems.

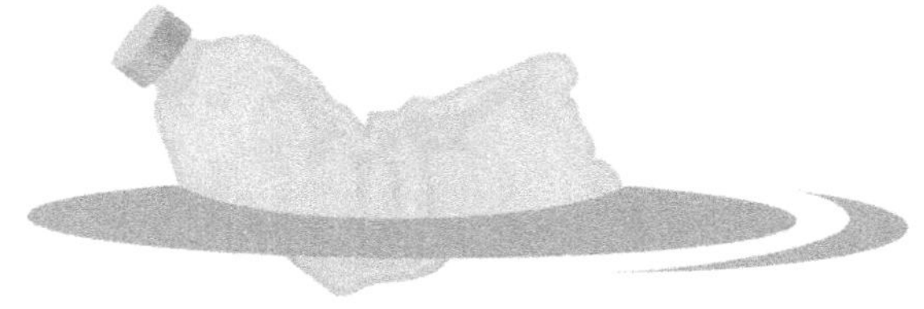

FUN OCEAN FACTS

- The ocean is home to underwater rivers and lakes, caused by differences in salinity.

- Bioluminescent bays glow at night due to tiny organisms that produce light.

- Sharks are older than dinosaurs, existing for over 400 million years.

- Sea stars can regrow lost arms and even grow a whole new body from a single arm.

- Some fish, like clownfish, can change gender depending on the social structure of their group.

- Sea otters wrap themselves in kelp to avoid drifting away while they sleep.

- Pufferfish can inflate their bodies to scare off predators.

- Some underwater volcanoes release boiling hot water, creating new ocean floor.

- The ocean is estimated to contain 20 million tons of gold, dissolved in seawater.

- The Bermuda Triangle, a mysterious area in the Atlantic Ocean, has many legends about disappearing ships and planes.

EARTH'S SECRETS

EARTH'S BASICS

- Earth is the third planet from the sun and the only one known to support life.

- Earth is approximately 4.5 billion years old.

- 70% of Earth's surface is covered by water, with most of it in oceans.

- Earth is not a perfect sphere; it's slightly flattened at the poles and bulges at the equator.

- The Earth's atmosphere is made up mostly of nitrogen (78%) and oxygen (21%).

- Earth has a magnetic field that protects us from harmful solar radiation.

- The Earth's crust is divided into tectonic plates that move and cause earthquakes.

- The tallest mountain on Earth is Mount Everest, reaching 29,032 feet above sea level.

- Earth's atmosphere has five layers, including the troposphere where we live.

- Earth orbits the sun at an average speed of 67,000 miles per hour.

GEOLOGICAL WONDERS

- The Grand Canyon in the USA is around 6 million years old.

- Mountains are formed by the movement of tectonic plates.

- The Mariana Trench is the deepest place on Earth, reaching about 36,000 feet.

- Diamonds are created deep within Earth's mantle under extreme pressure.

- The Dead Sea is the lowest point on land, at 1,410 feet below sea level.

- Earth's crust is broken into about 15 major tectonic plates.

- The longest mountain range is underwater, called the Mid-Atlantic Ridge.

- Volcanoes are formed when magma from Earth's mantle rises to the surface.

- Geysers, like those in Yellowstone, are caused by hot underground water shooting out of the ground.

- Earthquakes are most common around tectonic plate boundaries.

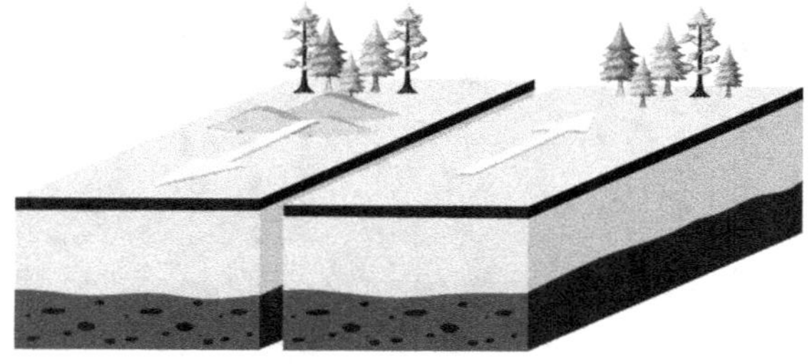

AMAZING ECOSYSTEMS

- Rainforests cover only 2% of Earth's surface but contain 50% of its species.

- The Amazon Rainforest is often called "the lungs of the Earth" because it produces so much oxygen.

- Coral reefs are the most biodiverse marine ecosystems on Earth.

- Deserts cover about one-third of Earth's land surface.

- The tundra biome is one of the coldest places on Earth, with permafrost soil.

- Wetlands act as natural filters, cleaning water and providing habitat for wildlife.

- Grasslands are also known as prairies, savannas, or steppes, depending on the region.

- Mangroves are unique trees that grow in saltwater and protect coastlines.

- The Great Barrier Reef is visible from space and is the world's largest coral reef system.

- The Taiga, or boreal forest, is the largest land biome on Earth.

NATURAL PHENOMENA

- The Northern Lights, or auroras, are caused by solar particles hitting Earth's atmosphere.

- Bioluminescence is a natural glow produced by some organisms in the ocean.

- Earth's gravity keeps everything, including the atmosphere, grounded.

- Lightning bolts can be hotter than the surface of the sun.

- Hurricanes, typhoons, and cyclones are the same type of storm, just named differently based on location.

- Rainbows are created when sunlight is refracted and reflected in raindrops.

- Tornadoes are rapidly spinning columns of air that touch the ground.

- Sinkholes form when the ground collapses due to water erosion underground.

- Glaciers are large, slow-moving rivers of ice that shape valleys and mountains.

- Volcanic lightning can occur during eruptions, caused by friction between ash particles.

MYSTERIOUS PLACES

- The Bermuda Triangle is a region where ships and planes have mysteriously disappeared.

- Stonehenge in England is an ancient structure with unknown origins.

- The Nazca Lines in Peru are large geoglyphs that can only be seen from the air.

- Easter Island is known for its mysterious statues called Moai.

- Lake Baikal in Russia is the deepest and one of the oldest freshwater lakes.

- Antarctica is the coldest, driest, and windiest continent on Earth.

- Devil's Tower in Wyoming is a massive rock formation with unknown origins.

- Blood Falls in Antarctica is a red-colored water flow caused by iron-rich water.

- The Sahara Desert was once a lush, green area with rivers and lakes.

- The Dead Sea is so salty that people can easily float on its surface.

EARTH'S HISTORY AND FOSSILS

- Fossils are remains of plants and animals that lived millions of years ago.

- The dinosaurs went extinct around 66 million years ago.

- Earth has gone through five major extinction events.

- The Cambrian Explosion was a period when many new species suddenly appeared.

- Amber is fossilized tree sap that can contain ancient insects.

- Pangea was a supercontinent that existed around 335 million years ago.

- The Ice Age was a period when glaciers covered large parts of Earth.

- The Permian Extinction wiped out about 90% of Earth's species.

- Fossils of sea creatures have been found on mountain tops, showing that they were once underwater.

- Palaeontologists are scientists who study fossils to learn about Earth's past.

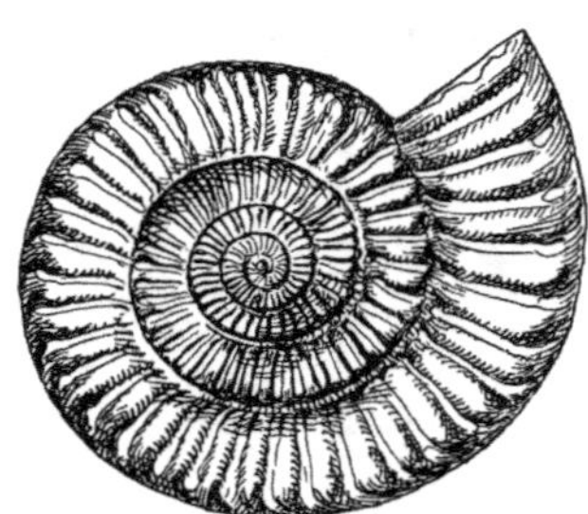

EARTH'S RESOURCES

- Gold, silver, and other metals are mined from Earth's crust.

- Coal and oil are fossil fuels, formed from ancient plants and animals.

- Natural gas is found deep underground and used as a fuel source.

- Earth's freshwater supply makes up only about 3% of all water on the planet.

- Salt is mined from the ground and also collected from evaporating seawater.

- Rare minerals, like lithium, are important for making electronics.

- Trees provide oxygen and absorb carbon dioxide, helping to clean the air.

- Soil is a mix of organic material, minerals, and organisms that supports plant life.

- Geothermal energy is heat from within Earth that can be used to generate electricity.

- Solar power comes from sunlight and is a renewable energy source.

EARTH'S WEATHER AND CLIMATE

- Climate is the long-term pattern of weather in a region.

- Earth has six climate zones: tropical, dry, temperate, cold, polar, and highland.

- Rainforests have the most rainfall of any ecosystem.

- Deserts get less than 10 inches of rain a year.

- Monsoons are seasonal winds that bring heavy rain to parts of Asia and Africa.

- Blizzards are snowstorms with strong winds and low visibility.

- Heatwaves are prolonged periods of extremely hot weather.

- Fog is a thick cloud that forms close to the ground.

- Hail is frozen raindrops that fall as solid ice during thunderstorms.

- Droughts are long periods with little or no rain, affecting water supplies.

EARTH'S CHANGING LANDSCAPE

- Erosion is the process by which soil and rock are worn away by wind or water.

- Mountains are formed by tectonic activity or volcanic eruptions.

- Valleys are created by rivers carving through land.

- Canyons are deep valleys with steep sides, often formed by rivers.

- Beaches are formed by the accumulation of sand and pebbles along shorelines.

- Sand dunes are mounds of sand created by wind in deserts and beaches.

- Volcanoes can create new land when lava cools and hardens.

- Islands are formed by volcanic activity or the movement of tectonic plates.

- Glaciers carve out valleys and create lakes as they move.

- Floodplains are flat areas that flood during heavy rains, depositing fertile soil.

FUN EARTH FACTS

- Earth is the only planet known to have plate tectonics.

- There are over 1 million known species of plants and animals on Earth.

- Earth's inner core is as hot as the surface of the sun.

- There are more trees on Earth than stars in the Milky Way.

- The Atlantic Ocean is getting wider each year due to tectonic plate movement.

- Earth has over 1,500 active volcanoes.

- Some rocks on Earth are over 4 billion years old.

- The Amazon River is the largest river by volume.

- Deserts receive less than 10% of the rain that rainforests get.

- Earth's longest river is the Nile, stretching over 4,100 miles.

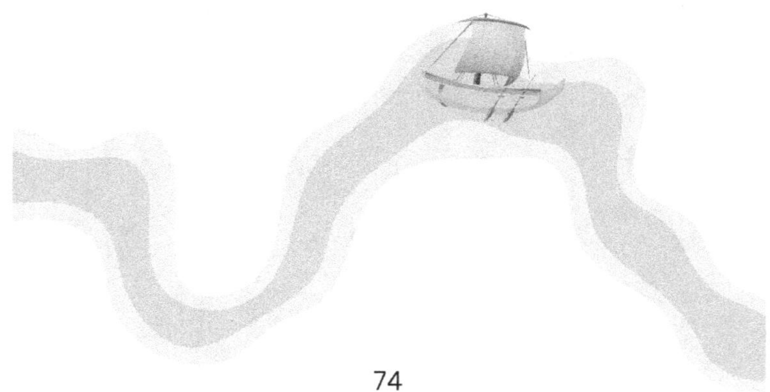

FAMOUS LANDMARKS

THE GREAT PYRAMID OF GIZA

- The Great Pyramid of Giza in Egypt is over 4,500 years old, making it one of the oldest structures in the world.

- It was originally 481 feet tall but has since lost some height due to erosion.

- The Great Pyramid is the only remaining structure of the original Seven Wonders of the Ancient World.

- Around 2.3 million stone blocks were used to build it, each weighing about 2.5 tons.

- It was built as a tomb for the Pharaoh Khufu.

THE EIFFEL TOWER

- The Eiffel Tower in Paris was completed in 1889 as the entrance arch for the 1889 World's Fair.

- It was originally intended to be dismantled after 20 years but was saved because it was useful as a radio tower.

- The tower stands at 1,083 feet, making it the tallest structure in Paris.

- It's painted every seven years to prevent rust, using about 60 tons of paint.

- The Eiffel Tower has over 1,700 steps, but most people take the elevator!

THE STATUE OF LIBERTY

- The Statue of Liberty was a gift from France to the United States in 1886.

- Lady Liberty stands 305 feet tall, including the pedestal.

- It's made of copper, which has turned green due to oxidation.

- Her crown has seven spikes, representing the seven continents and seas.

- Visitors can climb 354 steps to reach the crown.

THE GREAT WALL OF CHINA

- The Great Wall of China stretches over 13,000 miles, making it the longest wall in the world.

- Construction began in the 7th century BC and continued for centuries.

- It was built to protect China from northern invaders.

- The wall isn't a continuous structure but a series of walls and fortifications.

- It's visible from space, but only with the aid of telescopes.

THE COLOSSEUM

- The Colosseum in Rome was built in 70-80 AD and could hold around 50,000 spectators.

- It was used for gladiator fights, animal hunts, and mock naval battles.

- The structure has been damaged by earthquakes and stone robbers over the centuries.

- The Colosseum's original name was the Flavian Amphitheatre.

- It's one of the New Seven Wonders of the World.

MACHU PICCHU

- Machu Picchu is an ancient Inca city located in Peru, built in the 15th century.

- It sits high in the Andes Mountains at 7,970 feet above sea level.

- Machu Picchu was unknown to outsiders until it was rediscovered in 1911.

- The city's purpose is still debated, with theories suggesting it was a royal estate or a religious site.

- It was constructed without mortar; stones were precisely cut to fit together.

THE TAJ MAHAL

- The Taj Mahal in India was built as a mausoleum by Emperor Shah Jahan in memory of his wife, Mumtaz Mahal.

- Construction began in 1632 and took about 20 years to complete.

- It's made of white marble that changes color depending on the time of day.

- The Taj Mahal complex includes gardens, a mosque, and several other buildings.

- It's one of the most famous symbols of love.

THE SYDNEY OPERA HOUSE

- The Sydney Opera House in Australia was completed in 1973.

- Its unique design is inspired by the shape of sailing ships.

- It took 14 years to build and cost much more than initially planned.

- The building hosts over 1,500 performances each year.

- Its roof is made up of over a million ceramic tiles.

THE EMPIRE STATE BUILDING

- The Empire State Building in New York City was completed in 1931.

- It stood as the tallest building in the world until 1971.

- It has 102 floors and over 1,860 steps.

- The building is famous for its light displays, which change for different events.

- More than 4 million people visit the Empire State Building each year.

THE LEANING TOWER OF PISA

- The Leaning Tower of Pisa began tilting during its construction in the 12th century.

- It's 186 feet tall and leans at about a 4-degree angle.

- Efforts have been made to stabilize the tower to prevent further tilting.

- The tower is actually a freestanding bell tower for the nearby cathedral.

- It took nearly 200 years to complete the structure.

THE KREMLIN

- The Kremlin in Moscow, Russia, is a historic fortified complex that includes palaces, churches, and towers.

- It was originally built as a wooden structure in the 12th century.

- The walls are 20 feet thick in some places.

- The Kremlin is the official residence of the President of Russia.

- St. Basil's Cathedral is located just outside the Kremlin walls.

PETRA

- Petra is an ancient city in Jordan carved into rose-red cliffs.

- It was the capital of the Nabataean Kingdom around 300 BC.

- The city was lost to the Western world until it was rediscovered in 1812.

- Its most famous building is the Treasury, known for its intricate facade.

- Petra is a UNESCO World Heritage Site and one of the New Seven Wonders.

THE BURJ KHALIFA

- The Burj Khalifa in Dubai is currently the tallest building in the world, standing at 2,717 feet.

- It took six years to build, opening in 2010.

- The building has 163 floors.

- It's designed to withstand extreme heat and wind.

- The Burj Khalifa has a massive observation deck on the 148th floor.

ANGKOR WAT

- Angkor Wat in Cambodia is the largest religious monument in the world.

- It was originally built as a Hindu temple in the 12th century.

- The temple complex covers an area of 402 acres.

- Angkor Wat is featured on the Cambodian flag.

- The structure is surrounded by a large moat.

MOUNT RUSHMORE

- Mount Rushmore in South Dakota features the faces of four U.S. presidents carved into the granite.

- It took 14 years to complete, from 1927 to 1941.

- The faces are 60 feet tall.

- The site was designed to represent the birth, growth, and preservation of the United States.

- The presidents featured are George Washington, Thomas Jefferson, Theodore Roosevelt, and Abraham Lincoln.

BIG BEN

- Big Ben is the nickname of the Great Bell in London's Elizabeth Tower.

- It was completed in 1859.

- Big Ben chimes every hour, and its bell weighs 13.5 tons.

- The clock is famous for its accuracy.

- Elizabeth Tower leans slightly due to ground conditions.

THE PARTHENON

- The Parthenon in Athens, Greece, was built around 447-432 BC as a temple to the goddess Athena.

- It's considered one of the greatest examples of ancient Greek architecture.

- The Parthenon originally had vibrant colors and sculptures.

- It has survived earthquakes, wars, and explosions.

- It's made mostly of marble.

THE GOLDEN GATE BRIDGE

- The Golden Gate Bridge in San Francisco was completed in 1937.

- It's painted in "International Orange" to stand out in fog.

- The bridge is 1.7 miles long and has six lanes for traffic.

- It was the longest suspension bridge in the world when it opened.

- Around 10 million people visit the bridge each year.

THE SPHYNX

- The Great Sphinx of Giza is one of the world's oldest statues, dating back to around 2500 BC.

- It's 66 feet tall and 240 feet long.

- The Sphinx has the body of a lion and the head of a human.

- It was built to guard the Giza Plateau.

- The nose of the Sphinx is missing, and no one knows exactly why.

THE LOUVRE MUSEUM

- The Louvre in Paris is the world's largest art museum.

- It's home to the Mona Lisa and over 35,000 other pieces of art.

- The museum was originally a royal palace.

- The Louvre has a glass pyramid entrance, completed in 1989.

- Over 10 million people visit the museum each year.

DINOSAURS AND PREHISTORIC LIFE

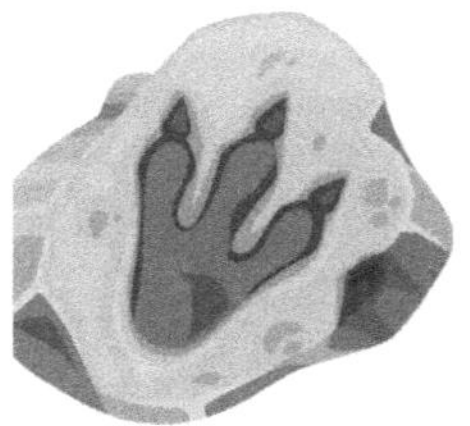

DINOSAURS

- Dinosaurs lived on Earth over 230 million years ago during the Mesozoic Era.

- The word "dinosaur" means "terrible lizard" in Greek.

- Dinosaurs lived on all seven continents, including Antarctica!

- There were more than 700 species of dinosaurs discovered by paleontologists.

- Dinosaurs are divided into two main groups based on hip structure: the "lizard-hipped" and "bird-hipped" dinosaurs.

FAMOUS DINOSAURS

- Tyrannosaurus rex (T. rex) is one of the most famous dinosaurs and had a bite force of over 12,000 pounds.

- Velociraptor was much smaller than shown in movies; it was about the size of a large turkey.

- Triceratops had three large facial horns and a frilled neck for protection.

- Stegosaurus had bony plates along its back, which may have been used for temperature regulation.

- Brachiosaurus was one of the tallest dinosaurs, with a neck that reached up to 40 feet in length.

SIZE AND WEIGHT

- Some dinosaurs were as small as chickens, like the Compsognathus.

- The Argentinosaurus is one of the largest dinosaurs known, estimated at around 100 feet long and weighing over 100 tons.

- Tyrannosaurus rex weighed about as much as a small airplane — around 9 tons!

- The average dinosaur was about the size of a small car.

- Many dinosaurs, like Brachiosaurus, were massive herbivores and ate up to 1,500 pounds of plants daily.

BEHAVIOR AND ABILITIES

- Some dinosaurs were capable of running as fast as 25 miles per hour.

- Many dinosaurs may have had feathers, especially smaller ones related to birds.

- Dinosaurs are closely related to modern birds, and some scientists believe birds are their living descendants.

- Dinosaurs laid eggs, and some even made nests to protect them.

- Some dinosaurs lived in herds, while others were solitary.

FOSSILS AND DISCOVERIES

- Dinosaur fossils have been found on every continent.

- Fossilized dinosaur eggs can be found in nests, sometimes with embryos inside.

- Paleontologists study fossils to learn about dinosaurs.

- The first dinosaur fossil was discovered in 1824 by William Buckland.

- Only a tiny fraction of dinosaur species are known, as fossilization is rare.

ANCIENT SEA CREATURES

- The oceans were filled with massive marine reptiles, like the Mosasaurus and Plesiosaurus.

- Megalodon was a prehistoric shark that could grow up to 60 feet long.

- Ichthyosaurus was a dolphin-like reptile that lived in the seas during the time of dinosaurs.

- Liopleurodon was a massive sea predator with sharp teeth and a powerful bite.

- The seas during the Jurassic period were rich with life, from ammonites to giant fish.

ANCIENT FLYING REPTILES

- Pterosaurs were flying reptiles and are often mistaken for dinosaurs.

- Quetzalcoatlus was the largest flying animal ever known, with a wingspan of 33 feet.

- Some pterosaurs had crests on their heads, possibly for display or balance.

- Pterosaurs are not classified as dinosaurs, but they lived during the same era.

- Pterosaurs likely had hair-like structures, which may have helped with insulation.

PREHISTORIC MAMMALS

- The first mammals appeared around the same time as dinosaurs.

- After dinosaurs went extinct, mammals became the dominant land animals.

- The woolly mammoth roamed during the Ice Age and had long, thick fur.

- Saber-toothed cats had long, sharp canine teeth, ideal for hunting.

- Glyptodon was a prehistoric, armored mammal, similar to a giant armadillo.

EXTINCTION OF DINOSAURS

- Dinosaurs went extinct around 66 million years ago.

- The leading theory is that a massive asteroid impact caused a global climate change.

- The impact likely created tsunamis, fires, and dust clouds that blocked sunlight.

- Only small animals, like mammals and birds, survived the extinction event.

- This extinction event marked the end of the Mesozoic Era and the rise of mammals.

ANCIENT PLANTS AND ECOSYSTEMS

- Ferns, cycads, and conifers were common plants during the time of dinosaurs.

- Flowering plants (angiosperms) first appeared during the Cretaceous period.

- Dinosaurs relied heavily on the plant life of their time, with herbivores grazing in forests and swamps.

- Fossils of ancient pollen and spores help scientists understand these ecosystems.

- The plant life of the time was crucial for the survival of herbivorous dinosaurs.

JURASSIC AND CRETACEOUS

- The Jurassic period came before the Cretaceous period, and both were part of the Mesozoic Era.

- The Jurassic period had a warm climate, with lush forests and swamps.

- The Cretaceous period was the last period before dinosaurs went extinct.

- Different types of dinosaurs dominated each period, with giants like Diplodocus in the Jurassic and T. rex in the Cretaceous.

- Some iconic dinosaurs, like Velociraptor, lived in the Cretaceous period.

DINOSAUR DIETS

- Carnivorous dinosaurs had sharp teeth for tearing meat, while herbivores had flat teeth for grinding plants.

- Spinosaurus may have eaten fish, as its teeth were adapted for catching slippery prey.

- Some dinosaurs had gastroliths, stones in their stomachs, to help grind up tough plant material.

- Sauropods were plant-eaters and ate enormous amounts of food daily.

- Dinosaur footprints show evidence of herding behavior in herbivores.

SPEED AND MOVEMENT

- The fastest dinosaur was likely the ostrich-like Gallimimus, running up to 30 mph.

- Some dinosaurs, like Ankylosaurus, had heavy armor for protection.

- Dinosaur tracks can give scientists clues about their behavior and speed.

- Theropods walked on two legs, while sauropods and ceratopsians walked on four.

- Dinosaurs likely used their tails for balance while moving.

DINOSAUR INTELLIGENCE

- Troodon is considered one of the smartest dinosaurs, with a relatively large brain.

- Many dinosaurs had good eyesight, possibly better than humans.

- T. rex had a strong sense of smell, helping it locate prey.

- Dinosaurs may have had complex social behaviors, especially herd-living species.

- Some paleontologists believe certain dinosaurs could communicate through sounds.

FOSSIL PRESERVATION

- Dinosaur bones often fossilize over millions of years, turning into stone.

- Soft tissues, like skin and organs, rarely fossilize.

- Amber can preserve small prehistoric creatures, like insects and plant material.

- Some fossils preserve the outlines of dinosaur skin or feathers.

- Fossils are found in sedimentary rock, formed from ancient mud and sand layers.

PLANTS AND ENVIRONMENTS

- Plants like cycads were common in the Mesozoic Era and are still around today.

- Ginkgo trees existed during the time of dinosaurs and are known as "living fossils."

- Dinosaurs roamed forests, deserts, swamps, and coastal areas.

- The breakup of the supercontinent Pangaea affected dinosaur evolution.

- Volcanoes were active during the dinosaur era, shaping the environment.

UNIQUE DINOSAURS

- Therizinosaurus had huge, clawed hands, possibly for defense or gathering plants.

- Microraptor was a small, four-winged dinosaur that may have glided between trees.

- Carnotaurus had tiny arms even smaller than T. rex's, with horns above its eyes.

- Hadrosaurs, also known as duck-billed dinosaurs, had hundreds of teeth for chewing plants.

- Ankylosaurus had a clubbed tail used as a weapon against predators.

DISCOVERIES AND NEW INSIGHTS

- New dinosaur species are still being discovered each year.

- Fossil footprints, or "ichnites," reveal dinosaur movement.

- Dinosaur fossils have even been found on the Isle of Skye in Scotland.

- Paleontologists use CT scans to study fossils without damaging them.

- Some dinosaur fossils contain traces of original proteins and pigments.

DINOSAUR EXTINCTION MYTHS

- Not all dinosaurs died during the extinction event; their relatives, birds, survived.

- There are myths that dinosaurs might still exist, like the Loch Ness Monster.

- Scientists believe that smaller animals survived by burrowing.

- The asteroid that caused dinosaur extinction hit near present-day Mexico.

- The "K-T boundary" is a layer of clay marking the end of the dinosaur era.

ONGOING MYSTERIES

- The exact colors of dinosaurs remain mostly unknown, but some evidence suggests feathers had colors.

- It's still a mystery whether dinosaurs had complex vocal sounds.

- Scientists continue to study dinosaur DNA but have not been able to bring any back to life.

- The full behavior of dinosaurs remains unknown, with many theories still debated.

- Dinosaurs continue to inspire discoveries and imaginations worldwide.

UNUSUAL WEATHER

TYPES OF WEATHER

- Weather is the daily condition of the atmosphere, including temperature, precipitation, and wind.

- Climate is different from weather; it's the average atmospheric conditions over longer periods.

- The Earth has five main climate types: tropical, dry, temperate, continental, and polar.

- Seasons are caused by the Earth's tilt as it orbits the Sun, creating varied weather across the year.

- Air pressure is a key factor in weather, affecting temperature, wind, and storm formation.

THUNDERSTORMS AND LIGHTNING

- A single lightning bolt can reach temperatures of 30,000°C, which is hotter than the surface of the Sun.

- Lightning strikes Earth about 100 times every second around the globe.

- Thunder is the sound created by the rapid expansion of air around a lightning bolt.

- There's a place in Venezuela, called Catatumbo, where lightning occurs almost every night.

- The Empire State Building is struck by lightning around 20 times per year.

TORNADOES

- A tornado is a rotating column of air that extends from a storm cloud to the ground.

- The U.S. has the most tornadoes in the world, especially in an area called "Tornado Alley."

- Tornado winds can reach up to 300 mph, faster than most sports cars.

- The strongest tornadoes are classified as EF5 on the Enhanced Fujita Scale.

- Tornadoes can pick up and carry animals and debris for miles.

HURRICANES AND CYCLONES

- Hurricanes, typhoons, and cyclones are different names for the same type of storm, depending on the location.

- The center of a hurricane, known as the eye, is typically calm.

- The strongest hurricane wind speeds can reach over 200 mph.

- Hurricane Katrina in 2005 was one of the costliest storms in U.S. history.

- The Pacific Ocean sees the most hurricanes, called typhoons in this region.

EXTREME TEMPERATURES

- The hottest temperature on Earth was recorded in Death Valley, California, at 56.7°C (134°F).

- The coldest temperature ever recorded was -89.2°C (-128.6°F), at Antarctica's Vostok Station.

- In desert areas, temperatures can change by over 30°C (86°F) between day and night.

- "Heatwaves" are prolonged periods of extremely hot weather, often lasting days or weeks.

- During a cold wave, temperatures can drop below freezing for extended periods.

UNUSUAL PRECIPITATION

- It can rain fish or frogs; this phenomenon is called "animal rain."

- Hailstones are balls of ice that form in thunderstorms and can be as large as a grapefruit.

- In 1887, a storm in Italy reportedly rained thousands of small fish.

- Blood rain is a phenomenon where red-colored rain falls, caused by dust or sand in the atmosphere.

- In some parts of the world, it can snow red or green snow, tinted by algae.

SNOW AND ICE

- Snowflakes have six sides and are all unique, but always symmetrical.

- Snow is not actually white but translucent, and it appears white because it reflects light.

- Some places, like Siberia, experience "diamond dust," which are tiny ice crystals floating in the air.

- The largest snowflake ever recorded was reportedly 15 inches wide, in Fort Keogh, Montana.

- Glaciers are huge masses of ice that move slowly over land, carving out valleys.

HEAT LIGHTNING AND FIRE WEATHER

- Heat lightning occurs on hot nights when lightning from distant storms lights up the sky.

- Wildfires can create their own weather, generating firestorms with powerful updrafts.

- Pyrocumulus clouds form over intense fires, creating clouds that sometimes produce lightning.

- Fire whirls are small tornado-like spirals of flames that can happen in intense fires.

- Dry lightning occurs without rain and can start wildfires, especially in dry climates.

SAND AND DUST STORMS

- Dust storms are common in desert regions, especially in the Sahara Desert.

- The Sahara Desert sends dust across the Atlantic, affecting air quality in the Caribbean and even the U.S.

- A haboob is a type of intense dust storm that can cover cities in minutes.

- Dust storms can reduce visibility to near zero, making it very dangerous to drive.

- Sandstorms can create temporary dunes in desert regions and reshape landscapes.

MONSOONS AND SEASONAL RAINS

- Monsoons are seasonal wind patterns that bring heavy rains to regions like India and Southeast Asia.

- The monsoon season is crucial for farming in many parts of Asia, as it provides most of the annual rainfall.

- Some areas receive over 400 inches of rain during the monsoon season, like Mawsynram in India.

- In Africa, the rainy season is called the "wet season" and is essential for crops and water supply.

- During monsoons, rivers can flood and create new waterways temporarily.

POLAR VORTEX

- A polar vortex is a large area of low-pressure cold air around the Earth's poles.

- Sometimes the polar vortex can shift, bringing extremely cold weather to lower latitudes.

- The polar vortex is strongest in winter, when the difference between polar and equatorial temperatures is greatest.

- When the polar vortex weakens, it can lead to sudden cold snaps.

- A split in the polar vortex in 2019 caused record low temperatures in the U.S.

UNIQUE CLOUD FORMATIONS

- Lenticular clouds look like UFOs and form near mountains due to air pressure differences.

- Mammatus clouds have pouch-like shapes, often seen during thunderstorms.

- Asperitas clouds have wavy, undulating shapes that look like an ocean in the sky.

- Noctilucent clouds glow at night, formed by ice crystals at the edge of the atmosphere.

- Cirrus clouds are high, wispy clouds made of ice crystals, often seen on sunny days.

RAINBOWS AND OPTICAL PHENOMENA

- Rainbows are caused by sunlight refracting in raindrops.

- Double rainbows occur when light is reflected twice inside water droplets.

- A full rainbow is actually a circle, but usually only half is visible from the ground.

- A halo is a ring of light around the sun or moon, caused by ice crystals in the atmosphere.

- Sundogs are bright spots that appear on either side of the sun due to light refraction.

EXTREME WIND

- Hurricanes, tornadoes, and typhoons all have powerful winds, but tornadoes have the strongest.

- A derecho is a powerful, long-lasting windstorm that moves in a straight line.

- The strongest non-tornado wind recorded was 254 mph on Barrow Island, Australia.

- Santa Ana winds are hot, dry winds in California that increase wildfire risk.

- The Chinook winds, or "snow eaters," quickly melt snow in the Rockies.

RARE WEATHER EVENTS

- Ball lightning is a mysterious ball of electricity that sometimes appears during thunderstorms.

- A snow thunderstorm, or "thundersnow," is a thunderstorm with snow instead of rain.

- Ice storms coat everything in a layer of ice, making for a stunning but dangerous landscape.

- "Cold air funnels" look like tornadoes but are not as dangerous, forming in cooler weather.

- In 2018, a rare "fire tornado" occurred in California, with winds over 140 mph.

IMPACT OF WEATHER ON NATURE

- Animals often sense storms before they arrive, possibly due to changes in air pressure.

- Birds sometimes get blown off course during hurricanes and end up in strange places.

- Coral reefs bleach when the water gets too warm, affecting marine life.

- Some insects and frogs only appear during rainy seasons, adapting to wet conditions.

- Landslides can happen after heavy rain, especially on steep or deforested slopes.

WEATHER-RELATED RECORDS

- The most rainfall in a single day was recorded in Réunion Island, with 71.8 inches.

- The deadliest tornado on record killed around 1,300 people in Bangladesh in 1989.

- The longest drought on record lasted 400 years, in the Atacama Desert in Chile.

- The windiest place on Earth is Antarctica, with wind speeds regularly reaching 200 mph.

- The world's largest hailstone weighed over 2 pounds, found in South Dakota.

WEATHER'S EFFECTS ON HUMANS

- Heatwaves are responsible for more deaths each year than other weather events.

- In ancient times, people thought gods caused storms and lightning.

- People in some cultures perform rain dances during droughts.

- Wind chill makes cold temperatures feel colder by removing heat from our skin.

- Humidity makes hot days feel hotter, because it prevents sweat from evaporating.

CLIMATE CHANGE

- Climate change is causing an increase in extreme weather events around the world.

- Arctic sea ice is melting at a rapid rate, affecting global weather patterns.

- Warmer oceans make hurricanes more powerful and increase flooding risks.

- Rising sea levels can lead to more severe storm surges in coastal areas.

- Deforestation can change local weather patterns by reducing moisture in the air.

STUDYING WEATHER

- Meteorologists use radar to track storms and predict weather patterns.

- Satellites orbiting Earth help scientists monitor hurricanes and other storms.

- The Doppler effect helps meteorologists track wind speed and direction.

- Weather balloons collect data from high altitudes, helping improve weather forecasts.

- Meteorology is the science of studying weather, which is constantly evolving.

FOOD FACTS

HISTORY OF FOOD

- Chocolate was once used as currency by the Aztecs; they valued cocoa beans so much they traded with them.

- Tomatoes were once considered poisonous in Europe because they're part of the nightshade family.

- The ancient Egyptians were the first to make marshmallows, using sap from the mallow plant.

- Pizza is thought to have originated in Naples, Italy, where people began adding tomatoes to flatbread.

- Potatoes were first cultivated in South America over 7,000 years ago.

FRUITS AND VEGETABLES

- Bananas are technically berries, but strawberries are not.

- Watermelons are 92% water, making them incredibly hydrating.

- There are over 7,500 types of apples grown around the world.

- Broccoli, cauliflower, cabbage, and kale all come from the same plant species—Brassica oleracea.

- Pineapples don't grow on trees; they grow from a plant close to the ground.

SWEET TREATS

- The most expensive chocolate in the world costs over $2,500 per pound.

- Honey is the only food that never spoils; it can last thousands of years.

- Cotton candy was invented by a dentist to make dental visits more exciting.

- Gummy bears were first invented in Germany in 1922 by Hans Riegel.

- It takes about 400 cocoa beans to make one pound of chocolate.

SPICES AND SEASONINGS

- Salt was so valuable in ancient times that it was used as a form of currency.

- Pepper was known as "black gold" and was highly valuable in the Middle Ages.

- Saffron is the most expensive spice in the world, costing thousands of dollars per pound.

- Vanilla comes from an orchid plant, and it's one of the most labor-intensive spices to grow.

- Cinnamon comes from the bark of trees in the Cinnamomum family.

AROUND THE WORLD

- Wasabi served in most restaurants is often just horseradish dyed green.

- The durian fruit is known as the "king of fruits" but smells so strong it's banned in many places.

- In Japan, square watermelons are grown to fit better in refrigerators.

- The largest pizza ever made was over 13,000 square feet, baked in Rome, Italy.

- In some parts of Thailand, people eat fried insects as a snack.

ANIMAL PRODUCTS

- Egg yolk color can vary depending on a chicken's diet—the more carrots or marigold petals, the deeper the color.

- Octopus is considered a delicacy in many countries, but in some places, it's eaten while still moving.

- Cow's milk isn't the only drinkable milk; people drink milk from goats, camels, yaks, and even reindeer.

- The eggs of emus and ostriches are much larger than chicken eggs and can weigh over a pound.

- Some people eat scorpions dipped in chocolate as a treat.

RECORD-BREAKING FOODS

- The heaviest pumpkin ever recorded weighed over 2,600 pounds.

- The world's largest chocolate bar weighed over 12,000 pounds.

- The longest sandwich ever made was over 2 miles long.

- The world's largest cheesecake weighed over 6,900 pounds.

- The largest cup of coffee ever made contained over 3,700 gallons.

STRANGE FOOD COMBINATIONS

- Peanut butter and jelly is a classic combo in the U.S., but peanut butter and pickles is popular with some, too.

- In Italy, pasta is traditionally never served with ketchup, but some people add it anyway.

- Some people put salt on watermelon to enhance the flavor.

- Creamy avocado blends well with chocolate for healthy desserts.

- French fries dipped in milkshake is a beloved combo for some people.

FOOD SCIENCE

- Carrots were originally purple until Dutch farmers cultivated the orange variety.

- Cutting onions releases a gas that irritates our eyes.

- Pineapples contain an enzyme that breaks down protein, which is why your mouth may feel tingly when eating it.

- The smell of fresh bread has been shown to make people feel happier.

- The sound of crunching food can make it taste better, according to research.

NUTRITIONAL FACTS

- Avocados have more potassium than bananas.

- Sweet potatoes are one of the healthiest vegetables, high in vitamins and antioxidants.

- Tomatoes are packed with lycopene, which may reduce the risk of heart disease.

- Almonds are technically seeds, not nuts.

- Bell peppers have more vitamin C than oranges.

BIZARRE FOOD LAWS

- In Singapore, chewing gum is banned to keep public spaces clean.

- In Italy, it's illegal to put pineapple on pizza in some areas, but it's more of a cultural taboo.

- In California, it's illegal to eat frogs that died in a frog-jumping contest.

- In the UK, there's a law requiring fish and chip shops to serve mushy peas with fish and chips.

- In China, it's illegal to waste food and not finish a meal in some cities.

FUN FACTS ABOUT DRINKS

- Tea is the most consumed drink in the world after water.

- The protein in milk calms the burn from spicy foods.

- Root beer is flavored with sassafras or sarsaparilla.

- In the 16th century, Europeans thought hot chocolate cured fevers and stomach issues.

- Coffee beans are actually seeds from a fruit, often called "coffee cherries".

BREAKFAST FOODS

- Pancakes date back to ancient Greece, where people made flat cakes with honey.

- Oatmeal has been a breakfast staple for centuries because it's filling and nutritious.

- Bagels are boiled before baking, which gives them their chewy texture.

- In Japan, rice and fish are common breakfast foods.

- Breakfast cereal was invented by Dr. John Kellogg, a nutritionist.

BAKING WONDERS

- Yeast is a living organism that makes bread rise by releasing gas.

- Some breads, like sourdough, can take days to make because of the long fermentation process.

- Baking soda helps cakes rise by creating air bubbles when it reacts with acids.

- Pavlova is a dessert named after a famous Russian ballerina.

- Croissants were actually invented in Austria, not France.

FAST FOOD FACTS

- Fast-food soda sizes today are over six times larger than in the 1950s.

- The first fast-food restaurant was White Castle, opened in 1921.

- In-N-Out is famous for its secret menu, where you can order items not on the menu.

- French fries were invented in Belgium, not France.

- The largest pizza chain in the world is Domino's Pizza.

CULTURAL FOODS AND TRADITIONS

- In Korea, kimchi is a staple food that's often fermented for months.

- In Italy, olive oil is a core ingredient in many dishes and is considered very healthy.

- In Ethiopia, injera is a type of flatbread used to scoop up food instead of utensils.

- In Thailand, the durian is a popular but very smelly fruit.

- In Japan, sushi is traditionally eaten with the hands, not chopsticks.

WEIRD FOOD FESTIVALS

- Spain holds an annual tomato-throwing festival called La Tomatina.

- In Italy, people celebrate truffles with festivals and fairs.

- There's an annual cheese-rolling event in England where people chase cheese down a hill.

- Japan has a "Natto Festival" to celebrate the sticky, fermented soybean dish.

- The U.S. has an annual National Pie Day, celebrated with pie-eating contests.

FOOD HEALTH BENEFITS

- Blueberries are known as a "superfood" because they're packed with antioxidants.

- Garlic may help reduce blood pressure and has been used as medicine for centuries.

- Dark chocolate has heart-healthy benefits due to its antioxidants.

- Ginger is known for helping with nausea and digestion.

- Spinach is rich in iron and great for energy.

FUN FOOD RECORDS

- The world's longest noodle was over 10,000 feet long, made in China.

- The biggest pancake on record was 49 feet in diameter.

- The most expensive coffee in the world is made from beans eaten and digested by civet cats.

- The record for the most marshmallows eaten in one minute is 25.

- The largest chocolate bar was created in the UK in 2011 weighing nearly 12,770 pounds.

UNUSUAL FLAVORS

- There's an ice cream flavor called "lobster ice cream" served in Maine, USA.

- Japan has KitKat flavors like green tea, wasabi, and soy sauce.

- People in some countries eat seaweed-flavored snacks.

- In Italy, there's a cheese with live maggots in it, called casu marzu.

- Jelly Belly makes "weird" jelly bean flavors like vomit and booger.

MYSTERIES OF THE DEEP JUNGLE

JUNGLE ECOSYSTEMS

- The Amazon Rainforest generates 20% of the world's oxygen.

- Rainforests cover only 6% of the Earth's surface but house over half of the world's species.

- The rainforest has four main layers: emergent, canopy, understory, and forest floor.

- Rainforest trees can reach heights of over 200 feet.

- A single rainforest tree can host hundreds of different species.

- The tropical rainforest is home to the world's largest living organism, a fungus in Oregon.

- Rainforest soil is actually very poor, and nutrients are recycled rapidly.

- A large number of rainforest species are still undiscovered.

- The Amazon Rainforest is about the size of the United States.

- Rainforest canopies can absorb 90% of sunlight and store it for energy.

WILD ANIMALS

- Jaguars are the largest cats in the Americas.

- A jaguar's bite is strong enough to pierce through turtle shells.

- The largest rodent in the world, the capybara, weighs over 100 pounds.

- Sloths spend up to 20 hours a day sleeping in the trees.

- Harpy eagles have talons that are larger than a grizzly bear's claws.

- The Amazon is home to pink river dolphins, one of the only freshwater dolphin species.

- Howler monkeys have the loudest calls of any land mammal.

- The tapir, a giant herbivore, uses its trunk-like nose to grab leaves from trees.

- Pygmy marmosets are the world's smallest monkeys, weighing only 4 ounces.

- The ocelot's coat helps it blend into the forest floor, making it a stealthy hunter.

JUNGLE PLANTS

- The Amazon rainforest contains over 16,000 tree species.

- The Amazon River basin hosts more plant species than all of Europe combined.

- The cacao tree, from which chocolate is made, thrives in the jungle.

- The rubber tree produces latex used to make rubber products.

- The ceiba tree can grow to over 200 feet and is considered sacred by many indigenous tribes.

- Lianas, thick vines that grow in rainforests, can stretch hundreds of feet to the tree canopy.

- The strangler fig wraps around other trees to gain access to sunlight.

- Bromeliads are unique plants that hold water in their leaves, creating mini-ecosystems.

- Some rainforest trees can grow roots that help prevent erosion and stabilize the ground.

- Rainforest plants produce many medicinal compounds that are still used by modern medicine.

JUNGLE INSECTS

- Ants in the Amazon can carry 50 times their body weight.

- Leafcutter ants are known for cutting leaves to cultivate fungus.

- Army ants can travel in massive swarms that overwhelm anything in their path.

- The bullet ant's sting is considered one of the most painful insect stings in the world.

- Dragonflies are excellent predators in the jungle, preying on mosquitoes and other insects.

- The Amazon is home to more than 2,000 species of butterflies.

- Poison dart frogs use bright colors to warn predators of their toxic skin.

- Termites build massive mounds that can be 10 feet tall.

- Moths in the Amazon have wingspans that can reach up to 10 inches.

- The Amazon is home to bioluminescent fungi that glow in the dark.

STRANGE AND UNIQUE CREATURES

- Electric eels can produce electric shocks up to 600 volts.

- The Jesus lizard can walk on water for short distances.

- Glass frogs are nearly transparent, allowing you to see their organs.

- Poisonous tree frogs get their toxins from their diet of ants and other small insects.

- The anaconda is the world's heaviest snake and can grow up to 30 feet long.

- A single colony of leafcutter ants can contain millions of individuals.

- Known for its incredibly slow movement, the sloth grows algae on its fur, which helps it camouflage in the jungle.

- The vampire bat feeds on the blood of other animals, including livestock.

- The bushmaster snake is one of the most dangerous snakes in the jungle, capable of delivering a lethal bite.

- The woolly monkey is one of the rarest primates in the world and is found only in the Amazon.

JUNGLE FACTS

- The jungle floor is almost completely dark due to the dense canopy above.

- Many animals in the jungle have evolved to be nocturnal to avoid the heat of the day.

- Some tree frogs use their skin to absorb moisture from the air, staying hydrated in the dry season.

- The largest rainforest in the world, the Amazon, produces its own weather patterns.

- Some trees in the jungle can "walk" by growing their roots outward to find sunlight.

- Certain plants in the jungle produce sounds to attract specific pollinators.

- The Amazon's canopy is constantly moving as trees grow, stretch, and lean.

- Some plants in the jungle release toxins to ward off herbivores.

- Rainforest species can be extremely specialized, living in one small area and relying on specific resources.

- The tropical rainforest is the world's most humid environment, with humidity levels over 90%.

ADAPTATIONS AND SURVIVAL

- Jungle animals often have camouflage to help them blend into the dense surroundings.

- Some jungle species, like the sloth, have slow metabolisms to conserve energy.

- Many animals in the jungle communicate using sound, with howler monkeys being particularly vocal.

- The dense foliage and canopy of the jungle protect animals from extreme weather conditions.

- Some plants in the jungle have evolved to be carnivorous, catching insects to survive.

- Jungle birds have bright plumage that serves as a warning to predators of their toxic nature.

- Rainforest animals, like jaguars, have sharp claws and teeth to help them hunt and defend themselves.

- The jungle's dense vegetation provides shelter for countless species, from tiny insects to large mammals.

- Many rainforest animals are arboreal, spending their lives in the trees to avoid predators.

- Some plants in the jungle have evolved to trap and digest insects for additional nutrients.

JUNGLE WATERWAYS

- The Amazon River is the second longest river in the world, flowing over 4,000 miles.

- The Amazon River Basin covers 2.7 million square miles, almost the size of the contiguous United States.

- There are over 1,100 tributaries of the Amazon River, many of which are home to unique species.

- Freshwater dolphins in the Amazon can navigate the murky waters with ease, using echolocation.

- The Amazon River is so wide in some places that it looks like an ocean.

- Piranhas, known for their sharp teeth, live in the waters of the Amazon River.

- The giant river otter lives in the Amazon and can grow up to 6 feet long.

- The Amazon Rainforest is home to a variety of aquatic plants, including floating lilies.

- The manatee, a sea cow, also calls the Amazon River home, living in the freshwater ecosystem.

- The Amazon has one of the most complex systems of freshwater ecosystems in the world.

JUNGLE PHENOMENON

- The forest floor of the Amazon is covered by a thick layer of decaying organic material.

- The tropical rainforest is the world's largest storehouse of carbon, helping to mitigate climate change.

- Rainforests have a constant, year-round growing season due to the warm temperatures and ample rainfall.

- The Amazon Rainforest helps regulate global temperatures by absorbing heat and moisture.

- Jungle creatures like ants and termites play a crucial role in decomposing organic material.

- Rainforests help to keep the global water cycle in balance, distributing water across the planet.

- Tropical forests are home to over 80% of the world's terrestrial species of insects.

- The jungle experiences heavy rainfall, with some areas receiving up to 400 inches of rain each year.

- The Amazon is a critical source of water for millions of people living in the region.

- Many animals in the jungle have adapted to live in extreme humidity and heat.

HUMAN CONNECTION

- Indigenous tribes have lived in the Amazon Rainforest for thousands of years.

- Some indigenous tribes use jungle plants for medicinal purposes, treating ailments like fevers and infections.

- The Amazon Rainforest has been called the "world's pharmacy" for its vast array of medicinal plants.

- The jungle plays a vital role in sustaining local communities by providing food, shelter, and resources.

- Many rainforest tribes practice sustainable farming techniques to avoid damaging the environment.

- The rainforest is under threat from deforestation, as logging and agriculture expand.

- The rainforest helps regulate the climate, which is crucial for the survival of all life on Earth.

- Environmental organizations work to preserve the Amazon to protect biodiversity and combat climate change.

- The Amazon Rainforest is essential for indigenous cultures and provides their livelihoods.

- Protecting the jungle from deforestation is key to maintaining global biodiversity.

FAMOUS EXPLORERS

EARLY EXPLORATION PIONEERS

- Marco Polo, an Italian merchant, is often credited with opening trade routes to China in the 13th century.

- Christopher Columbus believed he could find a new route to Asia by sailing west but instead discovered the Americas.

- Hernán Cortés is known for his conquest of the Aztec Empire in the early 1500s.

- Vasco da Gama was the first person to sail directly from Europe to India, reaching the Indian subcontinent in 1498.

- Ferdinand Magellan led the first expedition to circumnavigate the globe, although he died before completing the journey.

- Ibn Battuta, a Moroccan scholar, traveled over 75,000 miles throughout Africa, Asia, and Europe in the 14th century.

- Leif Erikson, a Norse explorer, is believed to have reached North America around the year 1000, almost 500 years before Columbus.

- John Cabot, an Italian explorer, is credited with discovering parts of North America under the English flag in 1497.

- Francisco Pizarro led the Spanish conquest of the Inca Empire in the early 16th century.

- Zheng He, a Chinese admiral, led seven major voyages across Asia and Africa during the Ming dynasty in the 15th century.

THE AGE OF DISCOVERY

- Prince Henry the Navigator, a Portuguese royal, established a school of navigation that played a key role in the Age of Discovery.

- Bartolomeu Dias was the first European to sail around the southern tip of Africa, known as the Cape of Good Hope, in 1488.

- Amerigo Vespucci, an Italian explorer, is the namesake of the Americas after his voyages to South America.

- Vasco Núñez de Balboa was the first European to see the Pacific Ocean from the New World in 1513.

- Sir Francis Drake, an English explorer and pirate, was the first Englishman to circumnavigate the globe.

- Martin Waldseemüller created the first map that labeled the Americas after Amerigo Vespucci's exploration.

- Samuel de Champlain founded the city of Quebec and is known as the "Father of New France."

- Sir Walter Raleigh led several expeditions to the Americas, including an attempt to establish the first English colony at Roanoke.

- James Cook is known for mapping the Pacific Ocean and claiming the eastern coast of Australia for Great Britain.

- Henry Hudson, an English explorer, navigated the Hudson River and discovered the region now known as New York.

ARCTIC EXPLORATION

- Roald Amundsen was the first person to reach the South Pole in 1911.

- Robert Falcon Scott led a British expedition to the South Pole, but Amundsen's team reached it first.

- Ernest Shackleton's endurance expedition to Antarctica is famous for his leadership during a harrowing survival story.

- Fridtjof Nansen, a Norwegian explorer, was the first to cross the Greenland interior.

- George Nares was the first to reach the Arctic Circle by ship and set the record for the longest polar exploration at the time.

- Matthew Henson was one of the first people to reach the North Pole in 1909, alongside Robert Peary.

- William Barents, a Dutch explorer, attempted to find a Northeast Passage to Asia and discovered the Barents Sea.

- Donald MacMillan, an American explorer, led several expeditions to the Arctic, conducting scientific research.

- Sir John Franklin led an ill-fated expedition to the Canadian Arctic that resulted in the loss of his entire crew.

- Vilhjálmur Stefánsson, an Icelandic explorer, led polar expeditions in the Arctic and studied the indigenous Inuit peoples.

AFRICAN EXPLORATION

- David Livingstone was a Scottish missionary and explorer who is famous for his exploration of Africa's interior and his search for the source of the Nile.

- Henry Morton Stanley, a Welsh-American explorer, is best known for his search for and eventual meeting with Dr. Livingstone.

- Mungo Park, a Scottish explorer, was the first known European to travel the length of the Niger River.

- Pierre Savorgnan de Brazza, an Italian-French explorer, played a key role in the French colonization of Central Africa.

- Richard Francis Burton, an English explorer, was the first European to see Lake Tanganyika and attempted to reach Mecca disguised as a Muslim.

- John Hanning Speke is credited with discovering Lake Victoria and identifying it as the source of the Nile.

- Alexandre Yersin, a Swiss-French physician and explorer, discovered the bacterium responsible for the plague while in Africa.

- Thomas Edison, while mostly known for his inventions, joined an African expedition to study the region's wildlife in the late 19th century.

- Mary Kingsley was an English explorer and writer who traveled extensively through West Africa, challenging stereotypes about women and explorers.

- Sir Samuel White Baker, an English explorer, discovered Lake Albert in Africa and helped chart parts of the Nile River.

EXPLORATION OF THE AMERICAS

- John Wesley Powell led the first successful expedition down the Colorado River through the Grand Canyon in 1869.

- Hernando de Soto led an expedition across the Southeastern United States and is credited with discovering the Mississippi River.

- Lewis and Clark, under President Thomas Jefferson's directive, explored the western portion of the United States, from Missouri to the Pacific Ocean.

- Cabeza de Vaca was a Spanish explorer who survived shipwrecks and wandered through the American Southwest for eight years.

- Alexander Mackenzie was the first recorded person to cross North America from the Atlantic to the Pacific.

- William Clark and Sacagawea were pivotal figures in the Lewis and Clark expedition, with Sacagawea serving as a guide and translator.

- Sir Alexander Burnes was one of the first Europeans to explore Afghanistan and parts of Central Asia.

- The Vikings, led by explorers like Erik the Red and Leif Erikson, are believed to have reached North America, particularly Newfoundland, around the year 1000.

- Zebulon Pike is known for leading expeditions to explore the southwestern United States and for climbing what is now known as Pike's Peak.

OCEAN EXPLORATION

- Jacques Cousteau, a French marine explorer, developed the first practical scuba diving equipment and explored the world's oceans.

- William Beebe, an American explorer, descended to 3,028 feet in the bathysphere to explore the deep ocean.

- Thor Heyerdahl, a Norwegian explorer, is famous for his Kon-Tiki expedition, where he sailed across the Pacific Ocean on a raft.

- James Cameron, the director of Titanic, also holds the record for the deepest solo dive to the Mariana Trench in 2012.

- Captain James Cook made extensive voyages in the Pacific Ocean, mapping many previously uncharted territories.

- Matthew Maury, known as the "Father of Modern Oceanography," mapped the world's winds and currents in the mid-1800s.

- Edward J. Smith, captain of the Titanic, had extensive experience navigating the North Atlantic Ocean.

- Neil Armstrong, the first man to walk on the moon, also had a background as a test pilot for ocean exploration programs.

- Sylvia Earle, a marine biologist, was the first woman to become the chief scientist of the National Oceanic and Atmospheric Administration (NOAA).

THE EXPLORATION OF SPACE

- Yuri Gagarin was the first human to travel into space, orbiting the Earth in 1961.

- Neil Armstrong became the first person to walk on the moon during the Apollo 11 mission in 1969.

- Sally Ride became the first American woman in space in 1983.

- Valentina Tereshkova, a Soviet cosmonaut, was the first woman to fly in space in 1963.

- Buzz Aldrin, an astronaut on Apollo 11, was the second person to set foot on the moon.

- John Glenn became the first American to orbit Earth in 1962 and later became the oldest person to fly in space at age 77.

- Chris Hadfield became the first Canadian to command the International Space Station.

- Hubble Space Telescope, named after astronomer Edwin Hubble, has transformed our understanding of the universe.

- Laika, the first living creature to orbit the Earth, was a Soviet space dog.

- Alan Shepard was the first American in space, flying aboard the Freedom 7 spacecraft in 1961.

WORLD-CHANGING EXPLORERS

- Charles Darwin's voyage on the HMS Beagle led to his theory of evolution by natural selection.

- Neil Armstrong's moon landing proved that humans could leave Earth and explore other worlds.

- Marco Polo's travels helped open up trade routes between Europe and Asia, increasing cultural exchange.

- Christopher Columbus' voyages helped establish the Columbian Exchange, changing the world's food, animals, and cultures.

- David Livingstone's African exploration contributed to the spread of European knowledge about Africa.

- Ferdinand Magellan's circumnavigation of the globe paved the way for global exploration and trade.

- Jacques Cousteau's oceanographic explorations revealed the rich ecosystems beneath the sea.

- Sir Edmund Hillary and Tenzing Norgay became the first people to summit Mount Everest in 1953.

- Alexander von Humboldt explored South America, becoming the father of modern geography.

- Amelia Earhart's solo flights inspired generations of women to enter aviation and explore the skies.

MODERN DAY PIONEERS

- Elon Musk's SpaceX is advancing space exploration with its reusable rockets and missions to Mars.

- Dr. Jane Goodall revolutionized the study of primates, becoming a leading expert on chimpanzees.

- Bear Grylls became famous for surviving extreme conditions in remote locations around the world.

- Ann Bancroft was the first woman to reach both the North and South Poles.

- Jacques Piccard's explorations of the deep ocean have advanced our knowledge of the ocean's depths.

- Tim Peake became the first British astronaut to live on the International Space Station.

- Ranulph Fiennes holds the record for the greatest distance traveled in the polar regions.

- Astronaut Mae Jemison became the first African-American woman to travel in space.

- Dr. Sylvia Earle has become a renowned advocate for the ocean, focusing on conservation efforts.

- Richard Branson's Virgin Galactic has pioneered the way for private space travel.

UNSOLVED MYSTERIES

- The disappearance of Amelia Earhart remains one of the greatest mysteries of aviation.

- The lost colony of Roanoke has puzzled historians for centuries.

- The fate of Sir John Franklin's expedition to the Arctic is still unknown, with many theories but no confirmed answers.

- The city of Atlantis, often referred to by ancient explorers, has never been definitively located.

- The lost treasure of the Incas, hidden after the Spanish conquest, remains a mystery to this day.

- The search for the Northwest Passage continues to intrigue explorers.

- The origins of the Nazca Lines in Peru are still a subject of much debate.

- The Easter Island statues (moai) continue to spark questions about the island's early inhabitants.

- The real story behind the Bermuda Triangle and the many missing ships and aircraft still fascinates explorers.

- The existence of a mythical city called El Dorado, said to be filled with gold, continues to inspire treasure hunters and explorers.

WEIRD SCIENCE

QUIRKY CHEMISTRY

- Water can boil and freeze at the same time under specific conditions known as the "triple point."

- There's enough DNA in the human body to stretch from the Earth to the Sun and back 600 times.

- Helium is the only element that can't be solidified by simply cooling it; it requires immense pressure.

- Gallium melts in your hand; its melting point is just above room temperature.

- If you pour liquid nitrogen into a balloon, it shrinks, but when warmed, it re-expands.

- Some metals, like sodium and potassium, can explode when they come in contact with water.

- There are over 10 million organic compounds, and new ones are discovered daily.

- Hot water freezes faster than cold water, a phenomenon known as the Mpemba effect.

- You can dissolve a pearl in vinegar due to its high calcium carbonate content.

- Some plastics can "heal" themselves when they are cracked or broken.

WONDERS OF SPACE

- Venus is hotter than Mercury, despite being farther from the Sun, because of its dense atmosphere.

- Space is so empty that sound can't travel there. If you screamed, no one could hear you!

- Astronauts can't burp in space because there's no gravity to separate liquid and gas in their stomachs.

- The Sun loses about 4 million tons of mass every second.

- On Mars, sunsets appear blue because of its dusty atmosphere.

- There's a "diamond planet" made of carbon called 55 Cancri e.

- Saturn's moon Titan has lakes of liquid methane instead of water.

- Neutron stars are so dense that a sugar-cube-sized amount would weigh a billion tons.

- The Great Red Spot on Jupiter is a storm that's been raging for at least 350 years.

- If two pieces of metal touch in space, they bond permanently due to the vacuum environment.

BIZARRE BIOLOGY

- Tardigrades, also known as water bears, can survive in space and extreme conditions like boiling water.

- Sea cucumbers can eject their internal organs to scare predators and later regenerate them.

- There's a species of jellyfish (Turritopsis dohrnii) that is considered biologically immortal.

- The blobfish looks normal underwater but appears "melted" when brought to the surface due to pressure changes.

- A kangaroo can't move backward because of its strong tail and body structure.

- Sloths only poop once a week, descending from trees for the event.

- The heart of a blue whale weighs as much as a small car.

- Some species of frogs can survive being frozen solid during winter.

- The immortal HeLa cells used in research were taken from Henrietta Lacks without her knowledge.

- Starfish don't have brains; their nervous system allows them to move and react.

STRANGE PHYSICS

- Time moves slower the closer you are to a strong gravitational field; this is called time dilation.

- Light behaves both as a wave and a particle, depending on how it's observed.

- A spoonful of neutron star material would weigh about 6 billion tons on Earth.

- The faster you move, the heavier you become due to relativistic mass increase.

- Lasers can trap and move tiny particles in what's known as "optical tweezers."

- You're technically younger when you spend time on a plane because of time dilation.

- A vacuum isn't completely empty; it's filled with virtual particles that pop in and out of existence.

- Sound travels faster in water than in air but slows down in solid objects like wood.

- You can levitate small objects using sound waves, a technique called acoustic levitation.

- Quantum entanglement allows particles to remain connected no matter the distance.

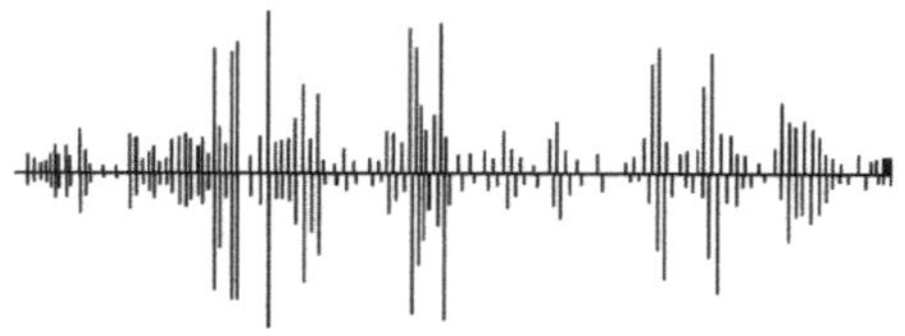

PECULIAR PLANTS

- The Venus flytrap closes its "mouth" in less than a second when triggered by prey.

- There's a tree called the "Tree of Life" in Bahrain that has survived in the desert for over 400 years.

- Bamboo can grow up to 35 inches in a single day.

- The corpse flower smells like rotting flesh to attract pollinators.

- Rafflesia flowers produce the largest individual blooms, reaching over 3 feet in diameter.

- Some plants "talk" by releasing chemicals to warn nearby plants of danger.

- The welwitschia plant can live up to 2,000 years in harsh desert environments.

- A tomato is classified as a fruit but is legally considered a vegetable in the U.S. for tax purposes.

- Touch-me-not plants fold their leaves when touched, possibly as a defense mechanism.

- Some orchids mimic female insects to attract male pollinators.

UNBELIEVABLE HUMAN BIOLOGY

- Your stomach replaces its lining every three to four days to prevent it from digesting itself.

- The brain uses the same amount of energy as a 10-watt lightbulb.

- Humans shed about 40 pounds of skin in their lifetime.

- A baby is born with about 300 bones, but many fuse together, leaving 206 by adulthood.

- You can live without a large portion of your liver; it regenerates itself.

- The human nose can detect over 1 trillion different scents.

- Human blood vessels could circle the Earth twice if laid end-to-end.

- Goosebumps are a leftover reflex from when humans had more body hair for warmth.

- The human body produces enough saliva in a lifetime to fill two swimming pools.

- Your brain generates more electrical impulses in a day than all the world's telephones combined.

TECHNOLOGY AND INNOVATIONS

- The first computer virus was created in 1986 and called "Brain."

- 3D printing has been used to create prosthetic limbs, car parts, and even food.

- The first email was sent in 1971 by Ray Tomlinson to himself.

- AI systems have written poetry that humans find indistinguishable from human work.

- Robots can now perform surgeries with extreme precision.

- Wi-Fi was invented by accident during a search for black holes.

- Self-healing concrete uses bacteria to repair cracks when water seeps in.

- Scientists have created artificial organs, including hearts, using 3D printing.

- The Large Hadron Collider recreates conditions from a trillionth of a second after the Big Bang.

- Nanotechnology can deliver medicines directly to individual cells.

NATURE'S WONDERS

- Lightning strikes the Earth about 8 million times per day.

- The Sahara Desert was once a lush rainforest.

- Honey never spoils; edible honey has been found in ancient Egyptian tombs.

- Lakes can explode under pressure from gases trapped beneath them, as seen in Lake Nyos.

- The Earth is hit by about 100 tons of meteoritic material every day.

- Spiders can survive underwater by creating air bubbles around their bodies.

- Fire whirls are rare phenomena where flames spiral like a tornado.

- Clouds can weigh millions of pounds, but their weight is spread out.

- Raindrops are not tear-shaped; they are more like hamburger buns.

- The deepest part of the ocean, the Mariana Trench, is over 7 miles deep.

CREEPY CRITTERS

- Some ants can create "rafts" using their bodies to survive floods.

- The mantis shrimp has the fastest punch in the animal kingdom.

- Octopuses can squirt ink and change colors to evade predators.

- Vampire bats can walk, run, and even jump.

- A cockroach can live for weeks without its head.

- Electric eels generate electricity to stun prey and defend themselves.

- Mosquitoes are attracted to carbon dioxide and certain body odors.

- A group of crows is called a "murder."

- Sea sponges are animals, not plants.

- Scorpions glow under ultraviolet light.

FUN FACTS ABOUT YOU

- Your brain can store an estimated 2.5 petabytes of information.

- A sneeze can travel up to 100 miles per hour.

- Humans share 60% of their DNA with bananas.

- The average person blinks about 20,000 times a day.

- You're taller in the morning because your spine compresses during the day.

- Your bones are five times stronger than steel of the same density.

- Fingernails grow faster on your dominant hand.

- The average human has about 67 different species of bacteria in their belly button.

- Tears contain a natural painkiller that reduces stress.

- Your body is made of stardust—most elements were formed in stars billions of years ago.

EXTRAORDINARY PLANTS

GIGANTIC WONDERS

- The giant sequoia tree can grow over 300 feet tall and live for more than 3,000 years.

- The Rafflesia flower produces the largest bloom in the world, measuring up to 3 feet in diameter.

- Bamboo is the fastest-growing plant, with some species growing up to 35 inches in a single day.

- The world's tallest tree, Hyperion, is a coastal redwood that stands at 379.7 feet.

- The Amazon water lily has leaves that can grow up to 10 feet in diameter and support small animals.

- Banyan trees can cover several acres with their sprawling roots and branches.

- The dragon tree produces a red resin known as "dragon's blood."

- Baobab trees, called "tree of life," can store thousands of liters of water in their trunks.

- The world's smallest flowering plant, Wolffia globosa, is smaller than a grain of rice.

- The quaking aspen tree forms colonies that can stretch for miles and is considered one of the largest living organisms on Earth.

CARNIVOROUS CURIOSITIES

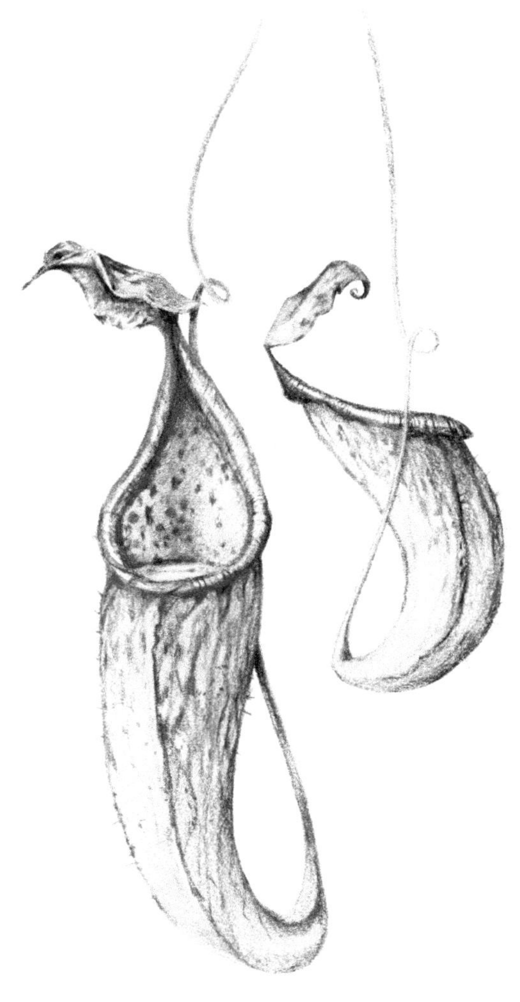

- Venus flytraps snap shut in less than a second to catch their prey.

- Pitcher plants trap insects in their liquid-filled pitchers, where they're digested.

- The sundew plant has sticky, glistening tentacles that ensnare unsuspecting insects.

- Cobra lilies resemble snakes and use nectar to lure insects to their doom.

- Bladderworts are aquatic carnivorous plants that suck in tiny prey with bladder-like traps.

- Butterworts trap insects on their sticky leaves and digest them for nutrients.

- Some pitcher plants form mutualistic relationships with bats, providing them shelter in exchange for nutrients from bat droppings.

- The Australian rainbow plant uses its sticky leaves to capture prey and provides food for ants.

- Carnivorous plants evolved in nutrient-poor soils to supplement their diets with insects.

- Nepenthes rajah, the world's largest pitcher plant, can trap small animals like frogs and mice.

UNIQUE SURVIVORS

- The resurrection plant can survive extreme dehydration and "come back to life" with water.

- Some cacti can live for hundreds of years in harsh desert environments.

- The welwitschia plant thrives in the Namib Desert and can live for over 1,000 years.

- Mangrove trees grow in saltwater environments and filter salt through their roots.

- Creosote bushes can live for thousands of years in arid deserts.

- The saguaro cactus can store up to 200 gallons of water.

- Ice plants store water in their leaves, making them excellent drought survivors.

- The puya plant has leaves so sharp that it can trap animals for nutrients.

- Arctic poppies can survive freezing temperatures and bloom in the tundra.

- The mountain avens thrive in rocky alpine environments with little soil.

MEDICINAL MARVELS

- Aloe vera has been used for centuries to treat burns and skin conditions.

- Willow bark contains salicin, a compound used to create aspirin.

- The Madagascar periwinkle is used to produce medicines for leukemia and lymphoma.

- The cinchona tree is the source of quinine, used to treat malaria.

- Ginseng root is prized for its energy-boosting and medicinal properties.

- Turmeric contains curcumin, a natural anti-inflammatory compound.

- The yew tree provides the compound paclitaxel, used in cancer treatments.

- Peppermint leaves are used to alleviate digestive issues.

- Lavender has calming properties and is used in aromatherapy.

- The neem tree is known as the "village pharmacy" in India for its many medicinal uses.

DEADLY BEAUTIES

- Oleander is beautiful but highly toxic to humans and animals.

- The castor bean plant produces ricin, one of the most poisonous substances on Earth.

- Belladonna, or deadly nightshade, was once used as a cosmetic despite its toxicity.

- The rosary pea's seeds contain a toxin called abrin, deadly in small amounts.

- Foxglove plants are toxic but are also a source of the heart medication digitalis.

- Angel's trumpet flowers are beautiful but can cause hallucinations or death if ingested.

- The manchineel tree produces a sap so toxic it can cause blisters on contact.

- Monkshood, also called wolf's bane, contains a toxin that can stop the heart.

- Poison ivy produces urushiol, which causes itchy and painful rashes.

- The death cap mushroom is responsible for most mushroom poisoning fatalities worldwide.

SENSORY SURPRISES

- Touch-me-not plants fold their leaves when touched.

- Mimosa pudica can "sense" light and move its leaves accordingly.

- The sensitive fern reacts to vibrations by curling its leaves.

- Cabbage plants release a chemical when chewed to warn nearby plants.

- Some trees "cry" by releasing sap when injured.

- Carnivorous plants can detect the struggle of their prey to trigger their traps.

- The peanut plant grows its pods underground after its flowers are pollinated.

- Pineapple plants can "hear" music, which may influence their growth.

- A Venus flytrap closes its trap faster when the prey struggles more.

- Some fungi glow in the dark through bioluminescence.

FOOD WONDERS

- Vanilla flavoring comes from the pods of the vanilla orchid.

- Chocolate is made from the seeds of the cacao tree.

- Breadfruit is a starchy fruit that can be baked like bread.

- Black pepper comes from dried, unripe berries of the pepper plant.

- Coffee beans are actually seeds inside the coffee cherry fruit.

- The durian fruit is banned in some places because of its strong smell.

- Carob is often used as a chocolate substitute.

- The baobab fruit is high in vitamin C and tastes tangy.

- Kiwis were originally called "Chinese gooseberries."

- Pineapples take up to two years to grow to full size.

"Chinese gooseberries"

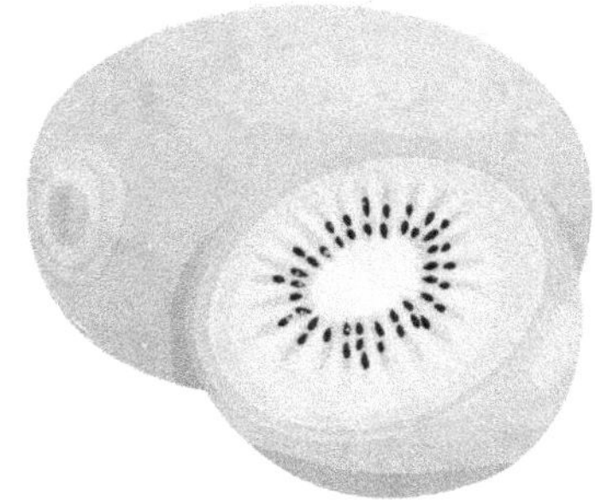

ANCIENT LEGENDS

- The Bodhi tree under which Buddha meditated is sacred in Buddhism.

- The coconut tree is called the "tree of life" in many cultures.

- Olive trees were a symbol of peace and prosperity in ancient Greece.

- The yew tree was considered sacred and connected to immortality by the Celts.

- The banyan tree is revered in Hinduism as a symbol of eternal life.

- The lotus flower is a symbol of purity in ancient Egyptian and Indian traditions.

- The "Tree of Tenere" was once the most isolated tree on Earth.

- In Norse mythology, Yggdrasil is a giant ash tree that connects all worlds.

- The cedar tree was used to build King Solomon's temple.

- Oak trees were sacred to Druids and often used for rituals.

FUN AND WEIRD PLANT FACTS

- Bananas are technically berries, while strawberries are not.

- Peanuts grow underground, unlike most nuts.

- The seeds of apples contain cyanide, but only in tiny, harmless amounts.

- Bamboo can survive extreme cold despite its tropical origins.

- Some fungi can take control of insects, turning them into "zombies."

- Trees communicate through underground fungal networks known as the "Wood Wide Web."

- Avocado trees need a buddy to produce fruit because they don't self-pollinate.

- Tomatoes were once called "love apples" and thought to be poisonous.

- Pine trees can produce seeds for hundreds of years.

- Grapes explode when microwaved due to plasma formation.

WONDERS OF THE MIND

AMAZING BRAIN BASICS

- Your brain weighs about 3 pounds—similar to the size of a cauliflower!

- The human brain is made up of about 86 billion nerve cells called neurons.

- Your brain is about 60% fat—it's one of the fattiest parts of your body.

- Even though it's small, your brain uses about 20% of your body's energy.

- A single neuron can send up to 1,000 messages every second.

- The brain sends and processes information faster than the speed of a race car!

- Every thought you have creates a tiny electrical signal in your brain.

- The brain has more connections than there are stars in the Milky Way galaxy.

- Your brain stays active, even when you sleep, to keep your body working.

- Babies are born with most of the brain cells they'll ever have.

- By age two, a toddler's brain is twice as active as an adult's brain.

- Your brain starts developing just three weeks after you begin growing in your mom's belly.

- Every second, your brain produces about 50 different thoughts.

- The left side of your brain controls the right side of your body—and the right side controls the left.

- It takes your brain only 1/10th of a second to recognize someone's face.

- Your brain doesn't feel pain—it has no pain sensors!

- About 75% of the brain is water—so staying hydrated helps it work better.

- The brain can store more information than a supercomputer.

- Your brain uses electrical signals to talk to different parts of your body.

- Even as you grow older, your brain can create new connections—this is called neuroplasticity.

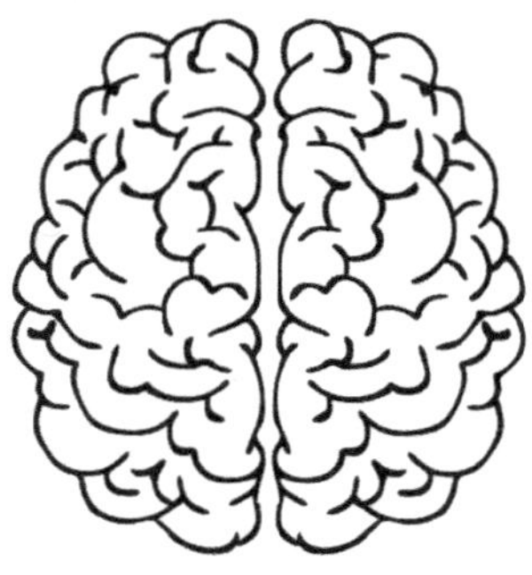

SENSORY SUPERPOWERS

- Your sense of smell is closely tied to your memories—that's why certain smells remind you of special moments.

- Your brain can identify thousands of different smells.

- It takes only a few moments for your brain to decide if food tastes good or not.

- Your ears send sound signals to your brain in the blink of an eye.

- The back part of your brain, called the occipital lobe, handles everything you see.

- People who are blind often develop stronger senses of hearing and touch.

- The average person can see about one million colors.

- Your brain "fills in the gaps" when you see incomplete pictures, which is why optical illusions can trick you.

- When you're in danger, your brain helps block pain so you can stay safe.

- The Brain Uses About 20% of Your Body's Energy to process sensory information.

- Your brain helps you figure out where sounds are coming from by comparing the sounds each ear hears.

- When light hits your eyes, your brain processes it so quickly that you don't even notice a delay.

- The human brain can sense even the tiniest bit of light in total darkness.

- Phantom limb sensation makes people feel like they still have a part of their body that's missing.

- Your brain thinks spicy food is a type of "heat," not a taste.

- Even when it's silent, your brain can "play" sounds you've heard before, like a song stuck in your head.

- Your sense of touch sends signals to your brain faster than the feeling of pain.

- Seeing familiar faces makes your brain light up with recognition.

- If you wear special glasses that flip everything upside down, your brain will adjust so it feels normal again.

- When you close your eyes, your brain can still detect light shining through your eyelids.

THINKING, LEARNING AND MEMORY

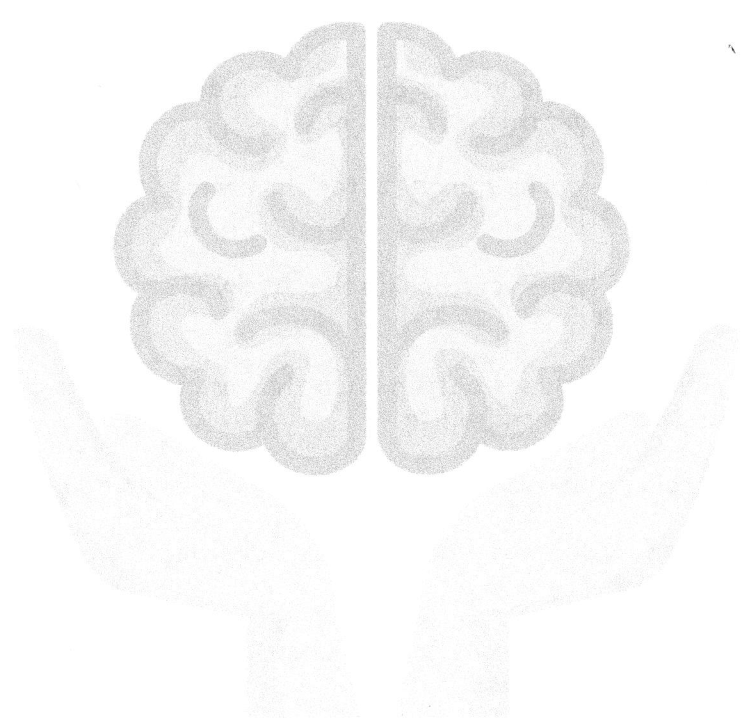

- Your brain can hold about 7 pieces of information at a time in short-term memory.

- Long-term memories are stored deep in your brain in an area called the hippocampus.

-

- Forgetting things helps your brain focus on what's important.

- Repeating things out loud helps your brain remember them better.

- Memories tied to strong emotions are easier to remember.

- Einstein's brain had lots of connections between its neurons, which helped him think creatively.

- Your brain re-learns things faster than when you learn them for the first time.

- Daydreaming helps your brain solve tricky problems in creative ways.

- You remember things better when they are written in color rather than black and white.

- Your brain organizes memories like a librarian sorts books.

- In just a few seconds, your brain decides what's worth remembering.

- You can train your brain to remember long lists by creating silly stories about them.

- Learning new languages makes your brain better at problem-solving.

- Studying hard makes your brain work like a muscle—it gets stronger!

- Most people forget their dreams shortly after waking up.

- Playing certain video games can improve your brain's ability to plan and solve problems.

- Exercise sends more oxygen to your brain, helping it work better.

- It takes about 21 days to train your brain to create a new habit.

- Sometimes, your brain just can't find the information it needs—this is called "forgetting."

- Reading stories strengthens the parts of your brain that help you understand other people's feelings.

EMOTIONS AND CREATIVITY

- Laughing uses five different parts of your brain all at once.

- Your brain releases feel-good chemicals when you laugh or smile.

- Feeling thankful activates your brain's happiness centers.

- The amygdala is the part of your brain that helps you recognize emotions like fear or joy.

- Your brain is most creative when you're daydreaming or relaxed.

- Both positive and negative emotions influence creative thinking in unique ways.

- Seeing someone else smile makes your brain want to smile, too!

- When you're upset, your brain releases stress chemicals to help you stay alert.

- Your brain lights up when you hear your favorite song.

- Bright colors in your environment can make your brain feel more creative.

- Your brain reacts to virtual reality the same way it reacts to real life.

- When you accomplish something, your brain rewards you with happy feelings.

- Writing by hand helps your brain remember things better than typing.

- Big ideas often pop into your brain when you're doing something simple, like taking a walk.

- Smiling, even when you're not happy, can actually make your brain feel better.

- Your brain remembers scary moments more clearly to help you stay safe in the future.

- Imagining yourself doing well at something can help you perform better.

- Your brain gets extra happy when you spend time with people you care about.

- Your Heart Beats in Sync with Your Emotions, speeding up when excited and slowing down when calm.

- Hugs release a special chemical in your brain that makes you feel loved.

MIND-BLOWING WONDERS

- Your brain creates enough electricity to power a tiny light bulb.

- When you're sleepy, your brain works slower than usual.

- During deep sleep, your brain stays busy organizing your thoughts and memories.

- Your brain can grow new cells, even when you're older.

- Multitasking makes your brain work harder, so it's better to focus on one thing at a time.

- Your brain notices movement faster than it notices still objects.

- Your brain can keep growing and learning new things, even after age 25!

- The size of your brain doesn't determine how smart you are— it's all about the connections.

- Some people train their brains to stay calm, even in tricky situations.

- When part of the brain is injured, other parts can sometimes take over and help out.

- Most of your brain's activity happens without you even knowing—it's called your subconscious.

- Your brain is like a detective—it can guess what will happen next based on clues.

- Quiet time or meditation can make your brain work more efficiently.

- Stress can make it harder for your brain to remember things, so relaxation is important.

- Sometimes, your brain makes up memories to fill in gaps.

- Déjà vu happens when your brain gets signals that make something feel familiar.

- Scientists think the human brain is still evolving and getting smarter over time.

- Brain freeze happens when something very cold touches the roof of your mouth, confusing your brain.

- Your brain can "copy" the emotions of others—this helps you understand how they feel.

- No two brains are exactly alike—not even in twins!

CREEPY CRAWLIES

INCREDIBLE INSECTS

- Ants can lift objects 50 times their own weight—like you lifting a car!

- Bees communicate with each other by dancing.

- Butterflies taste food with their feet.

- Some grasshoppers' legs can launch them 20 times their body length.

- Ladybugs can eat up to 5,000 aphids in their lifetime.

- A dragonfly can fly up to 35 miles per hour.

- Fireflies glow to attract mates and communicate with other fireflies.

- Praying mantises can turn their heads all the way around to look behind them.

- A group of butterflies is called a kaleidoscope.

- Cockroaches can live for a week without their heads (but only because they breathe through their bodies!).

- The world's smallest insect is a type of fairyfly, smaller than a grain of sand.

- Monarch butterflies migrate over 3,000 miles to escape the cold.

- Fleas can jump over 200 times their own body length.

- Ant colonies can have millions of ants working together like a big family.

- Dung beetles can roll balls of poop that are 50 times their weight.

- A single honeybee makes only 1/12 of a teaspoon of honey in its lifetime.

- Mosquitoes have been on Earth for over 100 million years—even dinosaurs dealt with them!

- Some beetles can spray stinky chemicals to defend themselves.

- Butterflies can't fly if their body temperature drops too low.

- Cicadas spend years underground, then emerge for a few weeks to sing and find mates.

SPOOKY SPIDERS

- Spiders aren't insects—they have eight legs, while insects only have six.

- Tarantulas can regrow lost legs when they molt.

- Jumping spiders have amazing vision and can leap 50 times their body length.

- Most spiders have tiny claws on the ends of their legs to grip webs.

- A spider's silk is five times stronger than steel of the same thickness.

- Spiders don't stick to their own webs because they step carefully on non-sticky strands.

- The goliath birdeater is the largest spider in the world, with a leg span up to 12 inches.

- Daddy longlegs aren't true spiders because they don't make silk.

- Some spiders build decoy versions of themselves out of web to trick predators.

- Wolf spiders carry their babies on their backs until they're old enough to hunt.

- Orb-weaver spiders create spiral-shaped webs that look like works of art.

- There's a spider called the "peacock spider" that dances to impress its mate.

- Some tarantulas can shoot tiny hairs to scare off predators.

- A black widow's venom is powerful, but they're very shy and avoid people.

- Spiders help humans by eating insects like flies and mosquitoes.

- Not all spiders spin webs—some hunt their prey on the ground.

- The diving bell spider lives underwater by trapping air in its web.

- Spiders have blue blood because of the copper in their bodies.

- Spiders sense vibrations in their webs to know when prey is caught.

- There are over 45,000 known species of spiders in the world!

AMAZING ARACHNIDS AND BUGS

- Scorpions glow under ultraviolet light!

- Ticks are arachnids, like spiders, but they feed on blood to survive.

- Centipedes have one pair of legs per body segment, while millipedes have two.

- The biggest centipede, the Amazonian giant centipede, can grow over a foot long.

- A millipede named Illacme plenipes has 1,300 legs—the most of any creature!

- Some scorpions can survive freezing temperatures by slowing down their bodies.

- The vinegaroon, also called a whip scorpion, sprays a vinegar-like liquid for defense.

- Pill bugs, or roly-polies, aren't insects—they're crustaceans like crabs.

- Roly-polies can drink water through their bottoms!

- Earwigs have pincers on their back end to protect themselves.

- The hissing cockroach makes loud hissing noises to scare off enemies.

- Bed bugs feed on humans while they sleep, but they don't spread diseases.

- Stick insects can grow over 20 inches long and camouflage perfectly with branches.

- Walking leaves look so much like real leaves that predators can't tell the difference.

- Some caterpillars mimic snake heads to scare away birds.

- Crickets chirp by rubbing their wings together—not their legs!

- Glowworms are larvae that glow in dark caves to attract food.

- Leafcutter ants carry pieces of leaves to grow a fungus that they eat.

- The rhinoceros beetle is so strong it can carry over 800 times its body weight.

- Some insects, like water striders, can walk on water by using surface tension.

AROUND THE WORLD

- The giant weta, found in New Zealand, is one of the heaviest insects on Earth.

- Madagascar hissing cockroaches are popular as pets because they're harmless.

- Bullet ants in South America have one of the most painful stings in the insect world.

- Leaf insects in Southeast Asia can lay eggs that look like seeds.

- In some parts of the world, people eat bugs like crickets and grasshoppers as snacks.

- The Hercules beetle, found in Central and South America, can grow up to 7 inches long.

- The Atlas moth, from Asia, has wings as big as a dinner plate.

- The Goliath beetle, found in Africa, weighs as much as a small apple.

- Army ants travel in huge groups and can eat small animals in their path.

- Termites can build mounds over 30 feet high—like skyscrapers for bugs!

- Water scorpions use a breathing tube like a snorkel to stay underwater.

- Bullet ants perform a "warning dance" to tell intruders to stay away.

- The Australian funnel-web spider has one of the fastest venom attacks in nature.

- Desert locusts form swarms that can cover hundreds of miles.

- The Brazilian wandering spider sometimes hides in bunches of bananas.

- Silk moths in Asia have been used to make silk for over 5,000 years.

- The assassin bug injects its prey with enzymes to turn it into liquid food.

- Bombardier beetles can spray boiling chemicals from their bodies to scare predators.

- Some caterpillars only eat one type of plant their entire lives.

- Certain spiders in South America use a "fishing line" of silk to catch small fish.

FUN BUG FACTS

- Insects have been around for over 400 million years—long before dinosaurs!

- Grasshoppers can make sounds by rubbing their wings or legs together.

- Moths are attracted to light because they use the moon to navigate.

- Ants leave scent trails so others can follow them to food.

- Butterflies can only fly when their wings are warm enough to work.

- Flies taste food by walking on it with their feet.

- The honeybee is the only insect that produces food humans eat.

- Termites chew wood but can't digest it—they rely on tiny helpers in their stomachs.

- Some dragonflies migrate thousands of miles, like birds!

- Mosquitoes are attracted to the carbon dioxide you breathe out.

- Certain spiders recycle their webs by eating them.

- Wasps can remember human faces and recognize friendly people.

- Caterpillars shed their skin several times before turning into a chrysalis.

- Some ants keep "pets" like aphids to milk them for sweet liquid called honeydew.

- The male luna moth doesn't have a mouth—it focuses only on finding a mate.

- Crickets chirp faster when it's warm outside.

- Fleas use their powerful back legs to jump huge distances for their size.

- Cockroaches can hold their breath for up to 40 minutes.

- Ladybugs can pretend to be dead to escape danger.

- Even though they're creepy, bugs help pollinate plants, clean the environment, and keep ecosystems healthy!

ROBOTS AND AI

WHAT ARE ROBOTS?

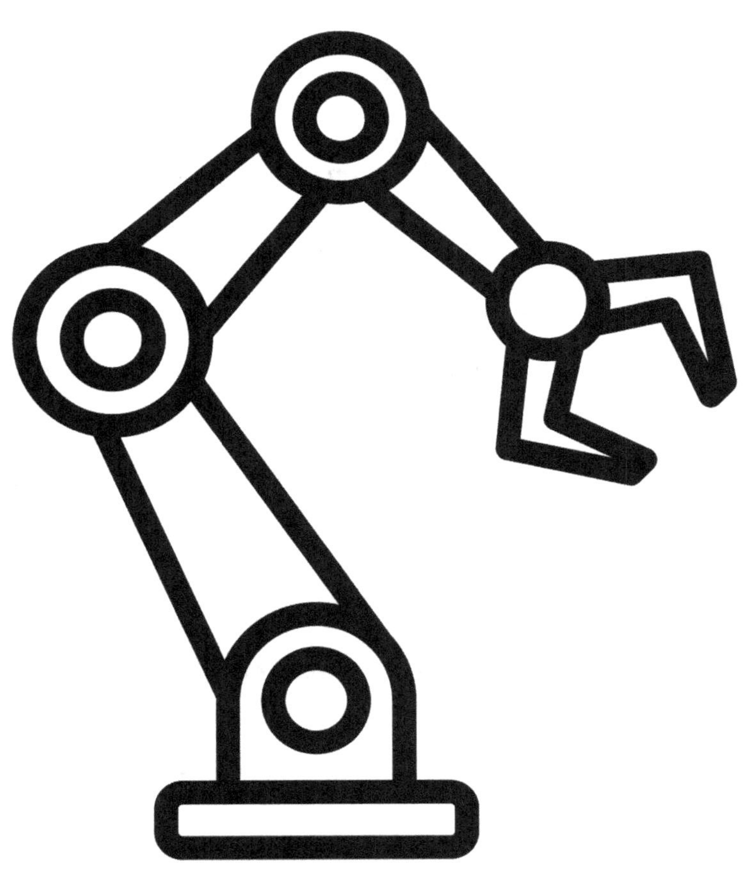

- A robot is a machine designed to do tasks that humans usually do.

- Robots can be programmed to follow instructions using computer code.

- Some robots look like humans, while others look like animals or tools.

- Robots have been used in factories for over 50 years to build cars and electronics.

- Robots don't get tired—they can work 24 hours a day without breaks.

- The word "robot" comes from the Czech word robota, meaning "forced labor."

- The first industrial robot, called Unimate, was built in 1961 to help make cars.

- Robots can explore places humans can't reach, like deep oceans or outer space.

- Some robots are as small as ants, designed to crawl through tiny spaces.

- Medical robots can help doctors perform surgeries with extreme precision.

- NASA uses robots like the Mars rovers to explore planets far away.

- Some robots are programmed to learn by copying what humans do.

- Robots with wheels are great for moving across flat surfaces.

- Some robots use legs to climb stairs or walk across rough terrain.

- Robots can have sensors to detect light, sound, heat, or even smells.

- Robots are used to clean up dangerous materials like nuclear waste.

- A robot can be controlled remotely or programmed to act on its own.

- Some robots can solve puzzles, like the Rubik's Cube, in seconds.

- Robots can help farmers by planting and watering crops.

- The tallest humanoid robot is over 13 feet tall!

HOW ROBOTS HELP US

- Robots help deliver packages in warehouses using conveyor belts or wheels.

- Some robots are designed to play music or act in movies.

- Robots can assemble tiny parts for smartphones and computers.

- Firefighting robots can go into dangerous areas to put out flames.

- Robots help clean skyscraper windows, even in strong winds.

- Underwater robots are used to study shipwrecks and coral reefs.

- Rescue robots help find people trapped after natural disasters like earthquakes.

- Some robots can translate languages in real time for travelers.

- Robots help detect and disarm bombs safely.

- Space robots, like Canadarm, assist astronauts on the International Space Station.

- Robots can be companions for elderly people, reminding them to take medicine.

- Robotic vacuum cleaners can clean your house while you relax!

- Robots in theme parks can entertain visitors with lifelike movements.

- Drones, a type of flying robot, are used for taking pictures and delivering goods.

- Police robots can investigate suspicious objects without risking human lives.

- Robots help scientists study volcanoes by measuring gases and heat.

- In hospitals, robots can deliver meals and medicines to patients.

- Some robots can 3D-print buildings or bridges, layer by layer.

- Robots are used in labs to run experiments faster than humans can.

- Delivery robots can bring food right to your doorstep!

ARTIFICIAL INTELLIGENCE BASICS

- Artificial Intelligence (AI) is the "brain" behind smart robots.

- AI allows machines to think, learn, and make decisions on their own.

- AI can recognize faces in photos and videos.

- Smart assistants like Siri and Alexa use AI to answer questions.

- AI helps predict the weather by analyzing tons of data quickly.

- AI can play games like chess and beat human champions!

- Some AI systems can write stories, music, or even poems.

- AI can detect spam emails and keep your inbox safe.

- Self-driving cars use AI to navigate streets without human drivers.

- AI helps doctors diagnose diseases by analyzing medical images.

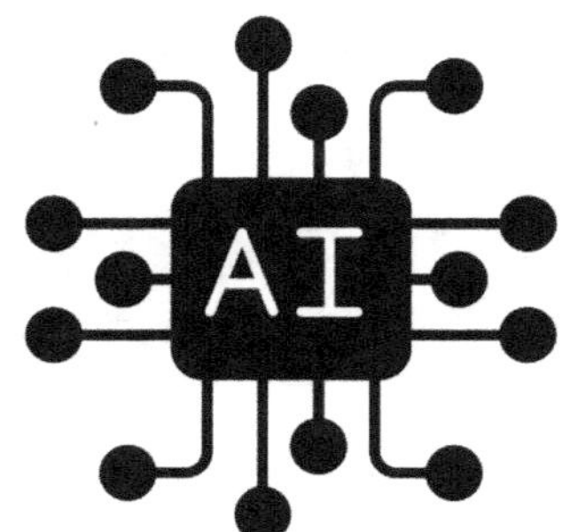

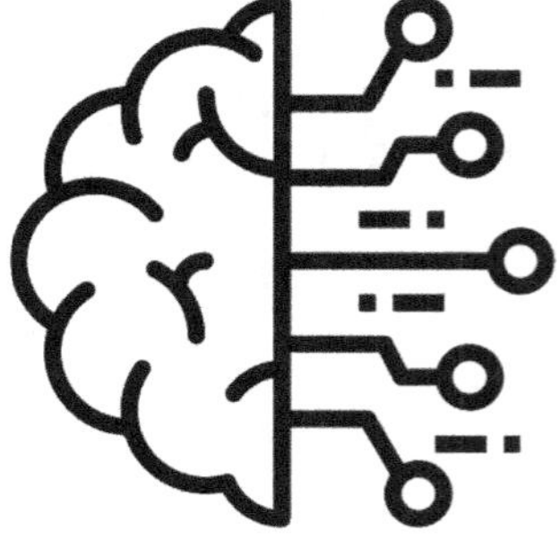

- AI can predict when machines need repairs to avoid breakdowns.

- Robots with AI can improve their skills by learning from mistakes.

- Chatbots use AI to talk to people online, like customer service helpers.

- AI can design video game characters that move and act like real people.

- AI programs can translate languages instantly for global communication.

- AI helps artists create digital drawings and animations.

- AI learns by analyzing patterns, like recognizing numbers or letters.

- Smart thermostats use AI to adjust your home's temperature automatically.

- AI can detect fake news by analyzing the reliability of sources.

- AI-powered cameras can follow moving objects, like athletes during a game.

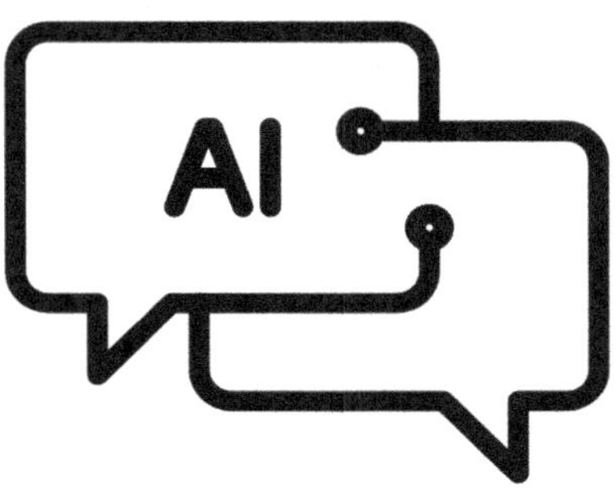

ROBOT AND AI ACHIEVEMENTS

- The Mars rover Perseverance uses AI to explore the planet and collect samples.

- Robots have been used to build underwater robots for ocean cleanup.

- The world's first AI artist, named AICAN, creates paintings for art galleries.

- The robot Sophia is famous for being able to have human-like conversations.

- AI helped map nearly all of the human genome, a blueprint of our DNA.

- AI systems can detect wildfires by spotting smoke from satellites.

- Boston Dynamics created a robot dog named Spot that can open doors.

- A robot in Japan named ASIMO can walk, run, and even dance!

- AI can sort recyclable materials in waste plants to help the environment.

- Robotic arms have built parts of rockets and satellites.

- AI has been used to predict the spread of diseases like the flu.

- Robots have helped clean up space debris in Earth's orbit.

- Robo-bees are tiny robots designed to pollinate plants like real bees.

- AI has created lifelike voices for virtual assistants and animated characters.

- Robots can play sports like soccer and even compete in tournaments.

- AI-powered telescopes help scientists find new planets in space.

- Smart robots are used to inspect and repair airplanes.

- A robot chef can prepare meals by following recipes!

- AI can create realistic animations for blockbuster movies.

- Robots are helping build roads and tunnels faster and safer.

FUN ROBOT AND AI FACTS

- Robots can perform surgery on grapes without squishing them!

- Some robots can fold laundry faster than humans.

- The first AI chatbot, named ELIZA, was created in the 1960s.

- Robots have been programmed to play instruments like drums and violins.

- The smallest robot, called a nanobot, is smaller than a grain of rice.

- AI can predict traffic jams and suggest faster routes.

- A robot named Curiosity has been exploring Mars since 2012.

- AI can compose songs that sound like they were made by famous musicians.

- Robots are even used to milk cows on farms.

- Self-driving delivery robots use cameras and sensors to avoid obstacles.

- AI-powered apps can turn photos into cartoons or paintings.

- The world's fastest robot can solve a Rubik's Cube in less than one second.

- Some robots use solar panels to recharge their batteries.

- AI can suggest books, movies, or songs you might like based on your preferences.

- Robots have helped scientists discover sunken treasure and lost cities.

- AI can identify animal species just by hearing their sounds.

- Robots are being developed to explore the Moon and Mars further.

- Some robots can play table tennis against humans—and win!

- AI-powered cars can recognize traffic signs and stop at red lights.

- Robots and AI are constantly evolving to make our lives easier and more exciting!